Contents

INTRODUCTION

VOR (Very High Frequency Omni Directional Radio Range) and ADF (Automatic Direction Finding) are the most commonly used radio aids for 'en route' and terminal area navigation. ADF is by many years the older of the two, and VOR was brought into use with the intention of replacing ADF. However, although VOR Beacons have grown like mushrooms, both along the airways and especially in terminal areas, the ADF Beacons have not faded away and are still very much a part of the air navigation scene, both as a secondary and primary aid.

As a practical example of where and when we might be required to use these 'navaids', as they are now called, we can look at a flight from GATWICK to BORDEAUX (Fig. 1). Instead of tracking on geographical features, we are flying from Radio Beacon to Radio Beacon. This is the basis of instrument navigation and a completely new world to the VFR pilot.

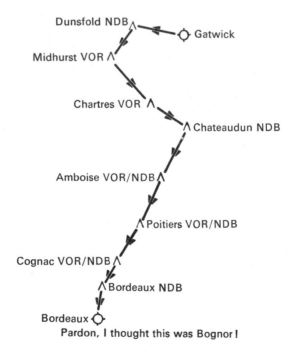

Pardon, I thought this was Bognor!

the VOR and ADF

Third Edition including DME

Martin Cass

Airlife

England

Copyright © Martin Cass 1977 & 1979

ISBN 1 85310 056 0

First Published 1977
2nd Revised Edition 1979
Reprinted 1988, 1989 and 1991

All rights reserved. No part of this book may be reproduced or
transmitted in any form or by any means, electronic or mechanical
including photocopying, recording or by any information storage
and retrieval system, without permission from the Publisher in
writing.

Although every care has been taken in the compilation of this book,
the Author and Publishers cannot be held responsible for any
inaccuracies or omissions therein.

Printed in England by Livesey Limited, Shrewsbury.

Airlife Publishing Ltd.

101 Longden Road, Shrewsbury SY3 9EB, England.

AUTHOR'S NOTE

This book has been written to give a comprehensive background for the understanding and use of the two radio aids. It is not in any way a substitute for practical training and instruction. The important fact to be remembered is, that to make full use of instrument navigation systems, it is necessary to hold an instrument rating. An I.M.C. rating is not the same thing, and, useful as it is, represents only a proportion of the training required.

The instrument descents into Guernsey and Jersey are included to give that extra depth of understanding to the basic exercises, and as an introduction to the more advanced techniques. It would be illegal to carry out a flight in a control zone in bad weather unless you could accept an IFR clearance, and this you cannot do without an I/R. It is also dangerous to put yourself in a situation which requires skills beyond your training and capabilities. Always err on the side of caution and make sure that the weather does not catch you out.

"It is better to be down here, wishing you were up there, than up there, wishing you were down here".

Many of us imagine that the possession of these aids heralds a future of mindless ease as we tune in and await the appearance of our destination. This is far from true, but armed with knowledge, practical experience and an awareness of their errors and pitfalls we can make our flying much easier and more relaxed. We may be unsure of our position yet still know that we are on the right track. Used to their fullest extent we can, without reference to the ground, keep a continuous picture of our position and progress, simply by reading and interpreting the cockpit instruments in conjunction with a chart and combining this with a certain amount of elementary deduction. Both VOR and ADF have operational limitations and are subject to a number of possible errors. Like all instruments they are capable of being misread by the pilot. Even worse, they can mislead the pilot into following an erroneous course of action. Thus a well-equipped flight panel means a lot more work and understanding before its advantages can be used with safety. Having learnt how to switch the set on, does not teach us how to use it, and to some extent we must regard the acquisition of each lesson in the same way. In other words, do not assume that because you have, by some miracle, set course from VOR "A" and arrived at your planned destination NDB "X", (NDB is another way of describing ADF, NDB meaning Non-Directional Beacon), that you have fully mastered the art, from switch on—to instrument let down. You have not, and will not, unless you realise that each lesson is a step towards the whole, which, in turn, requires proper training and experience.

Radio Navigation is carried out in conjunction with Radio Navigation charts, but in the early stages you may use the half million topographical maps. These are quite sufficient for VMC/VFR Radio Navigation and as well as being used to them they give you a much better idea of terrain heights and geographical features. Full IFR/IMC Radio Navigation must be carried out from specialised radio charts.

In times past it was rare for a Club training aircraft to be equipped with either of these radio aids. Now, it is considered almost a necessity to have at least a VOR. In fact in the case of a VFR flight to Le Bourget, for instance, it is only possible to follow the required VFR tracks and find the VFR reporting points accurately with the assistance of VOR. It is most likely that during the next few years, with the lead taken by the Continent, VFR flights in controlled airspace will be impossible without VOR and eventually DME (Distance Measuring Equipment) as well.

The VOR

1. HOW DO WE FIND THE LOCATION OF A VOR STATION?

If you look at the ½ million map of Southern England, and find Seaford, which is a little to the west of Eastbourne, you will see that there is a small six sided symbol surrounded by a rather large compass rose. This is a VOR position marker. Looking around further, you will see that the South East corner of England is well supplied with them. In fact, there are some sixteen VOR stations, which are tuneable and useable from overhead Gatwick or Heathrow. As an example of a VOR on the Northern England map, there is Pole Hill, between Bradford and Manchester.

2. WHAT INFORMATION IS SHOWN ON THE CHART?

1. The frequency 117.0 (VOR's transmit on frequencies between 112 Mc/s and 118 Mc/s). 117.0 is the frequency for the Seaford beacon.
2. The name and call sign of the station: SEAFORD. The letters of the call sign or morse indent are underlined (SFD).
3. Magnetic North and the other cardinal points are shown by numbered arrows. 30° intervals are given longer lines than the remaining 10° intervals.

FIG.2

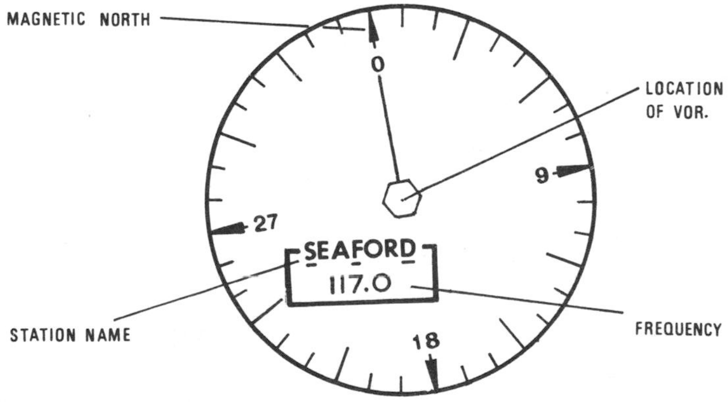

1

3. WHY IS THE VOR SIGNAL ORIENTATED WITH LOCAL MAGNETIC NORTH?

As we steer by a direction indicator, which is synchronised with a magnetic compass, it is convenient to use magnetic information, rather than true.

4. HOW DOES THE GROUND STATION WORK?

Apart from some exotic new type doppler VOR's, which look similar to an enormous birthday cake, the humble, ordinary VOR is usually housed in a round blockhouse structure.

The equipment is installed in a reasonably flat, open space, such as an airport, large meadow or lonely hill top. The transmissions are made in the VHF band, between 112 Mc/s and 118 Mc/s, so it has the same line of sight characteristics as the VHF communication set.

The principle is, that it can indicate to the airborne receiver the whereabouts of the aircraft, in relation to the magnetic 360° radial of the ground station. Thus the ground station transmits an omni-directional signal, followed by a rotating directional signal. The receiver then carries out a phase comparison in time, between the reception of the first signal and the arrival of the rotating signal. The difference is electrically translated into the number of degrees from magnetic north. If there was no time difference between the signals, then they are said to be in phase, and the aircraft is somewhere along the Magnetic North radial. If the phase difference is 130° then this indicates that the aircraft is along the 130° radial from the station, and so on. The equipment is designed to give any radial from 0° − 359°. (See Fig. 4).

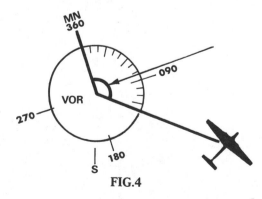

FIG.4

5. HOW DO WE OPERATE THE AIRBORNE EQUIPMENT AND WHAT DOES IT CONSIST OF?

The airborne equipment consists of a V shaped aerial, a receiver and an indicator unit. The receiver will either have its own on/off switch, or be coupled with the communication set. It will also have a switch position, to bring in the 3 letter morse identification signal.

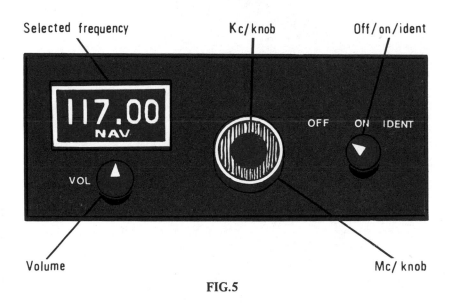

Selected frequency   Kc/knob   Off/on/ident

VOL   OFF   ON   IDENT

117.00
NAV.

Volume   Mc/knob

FIG.5

The indicator varies considerably from type to type, but the basis is the same for all of them: a round dial, with the compass rose on the outer rim and an OBS (omni bearing selector) knob, with which to select the required bearing. The selected radial may appear at the bottom or top of the dial according to the make, so ensure you understand your own equipment. The reciprocal of the selected bearing is usually shown in the opposite window. (See Fig. 6).

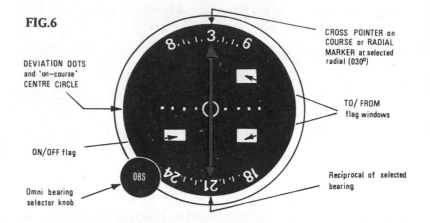

FIG.6

DEVIATION DOTS
and 'on—course'
CENTRE CIRCLE

ON/OFF flag

Omni bearing
selector knob

CROSS POINTER on
COURSE or RADIAL
MARKER at selected
radial (030°)

TO/ FROM
flag windows

Reciprocal of selected
bearing

The needle pointer pivoted at the top centre of the instrument face has several recognised titles:—

Deviation indicator
Course indicator
Cross pointer

We shall use the term 'Cross pointer' to describe it. This needle is pivoted at the top and is free to move from the 'on course' centre circle to the left or the right of the instrument dial. It tells us, in a straightforward manner, whether or not we are on the selected track, and if we are not, which way to turn to regain the track. The centre circle is the 'on course' area of the dial. The dots on either side of it each represent two and a half degrees ($2\frac{1}{2}°$), so that full scale deflection of the pointer occurs when the aircraft is displaced by $10°$ or more, from the selected radial.

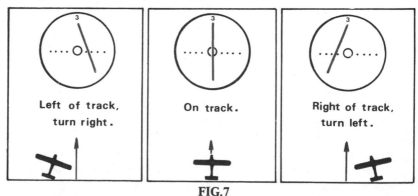

Left of track, turn right.	On track.	Right of track, turn left.

FIG.7

The To/From flags give the pilot an immediate indication of which side of the station the aircraft is positioned with relation to the selected radial. For example, with the radial 359° selected we want to know whether we will fly towards or away from the station when steering and maintaining this course. By knowing this, we also have an indication of our geographical position with relation to the station.

The VOR indicates this by resolving radial, and radial reciprocal into "to/from" indications. If the aircraft is nearer the selected radial than its reciprocal, then the 'FROM' flag will show. If the aircraft is nearer the reciprocal of the selected radial then the 'TO' flag will show. (See Fig. 8).

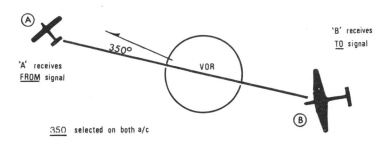

FIG.8

The ON/OFF flag shows red, or off when the set is:—
(a)   switched off
(b)   the set is switched on, but the signal strength is not sufficient to be relied on
(c)   the set is switched on, but the equipment is faulty
(d)   the set is switched on, but the aircraft is in an area approximately 90° from the selected radial.

Using the VOR

The radials, or bearings, fan out from the VOR station like the imaginary spokes of a wheel, 360 of them, each one representing one degree. The nearer we are to the VOR station, the quicker we cross the radials, or the more likely we are to wander from one radial to another. We soon realise that the cross pointer becomes exceedingly lively the nearer we are to the station and becomes rather more leisurely with distance.

5

The 1 in 60 rule applies to VOR radials in the same way as it does to track error problems. If we are 1 mile off course at a distance of 60 miles, then we should alter heading by 1^O to prevent further track error. At 30 miles from the beacon your track will be in error by 2^O for every mile of track deviation. At 10 miles the same error equals 6°. At 60 miles the width of 1 radial is about 1 NM, at 10 miles the width is reduced to 1,000ft This is why it gets more difficult to hold the VOR track as we get nearer the station and why the aircraft crosses the radials at a much greater rate. Overhead the beacon we will intercept all the radials at once.

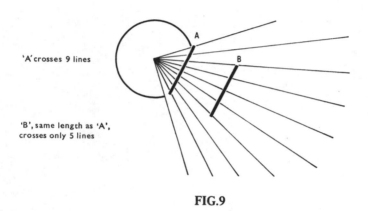

'A' crosses 9 lines

'B', same length as 'A', crosses only 5 lines

FIG.9

SEQUENCE 1: TUNING THE SET

(1) Switch on the set.
(2) Select the frequency of the VOR station required.
(3) Check that you have selected the correct frequency.
(4) Ensure that the off flag has disappeared.
(5) Turn up the volume and identify the morse signal.
(6) Turn the OBS through 360° and ensure that the cross pointer swings across the dial face, twice, and that the TO/FROM flags appear in turn in their respective windows.
(7) Turn the OBS until the cross pointer is centred, note whether the TO or FROM flag is showing, and check that the bearing agrees with the known or approximate position of the aircraft.
(8) If you are satisfied that the correct VOR has been selected and the equipment is working, turn down the ident signal.

FAULTS

1. **Incorrect frequency.**
2. **VOR station switched off. This happens at least once a month for about 2 hours, when the equipment is being serviced. Times and dates can be found in the Air Pilot, or recognised flight guides.**
3. **Ground station unserviceable.**
4. **Airborne equipment unserviceable.**

A sure sign that we are too low, or too faraway, is the failure of the "on" flag to show, or the cross pointer to give definite indications.

Again, the signals will not be received satisfactorily if there is high terrain between us and the selected station. Apart from these two restrictions VOR is not subject to the numerous errors of the ADF.

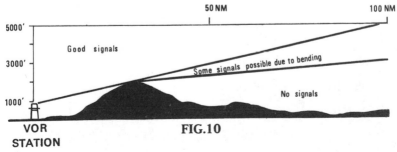

FIG.10

SEQUENCE 2: FINDING THE DIRECT MAGNETIC TRACK TO THE STATION

NOTE: The heading of the aircraft is immaterial, the bearing will be the same for all aircraft on the same radial (See Fig. 11).

FIG.11 *The same aircraft would also get 270° "FROM" WHICH is the RECIPROCAL OF 090°.*

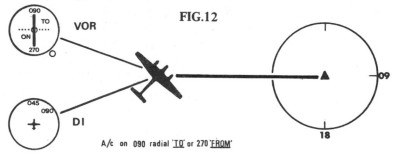

(1) Tune and identify station.

(2) Turn OBS until the cross pointer is centred and the "TO" flag is showing in the window.

(3) Read against the course marker (at the top of the dial in most instruments), the magnetic track to the station.

(4) If you wish to draw this track on the "topographical" chart: just read off the reciprocal bearing at the bottom of the dial and draw this track from the VOR, on the map. (See Fig. 12).

FIG.12

A/c on 090 radial 'TO' or 270 'FROM'

It is important to note that strictly speaking we are on the 270° radial from the station and not the 090° "to". This is because all radials are from the station, but as the equipment can translate this instantly into TO or FROM, we can simply consider it as track "TO" or "FROM", or "bearing" to or from.

By turning the OBS until 27 is at the top of the VOR dial, the "TO" signal will disappear and the "FROM" flag will appear.

SEQUENCE 3: FINDING THE MAGNETIC BEARING FROM THE STATION

(1) Tune and identify.
(2) Turn OBS until the cross pointer is centred and the "FROM" flag is showing in the window.
(3) Read the bearing from the station, at the top of the dial.

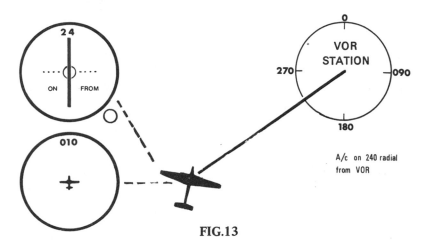

FIG.13

The aircraft is heading 010° and is crossing the 240° radial from the VOR. If we turn the OBS until the pointer is centred and the "TO" flag is in the window, instead of the "FROM" flag, then the QDM of 060° will be indicated at the top.

(4) We can now project the 240° radial from the VOR's location, and we are somewhere along this line. With the aid of a map and a rough idea of which county we are in, we ought to be able to find our position. Using another VOR or ADF we can pinpoint our position with reasonable accuracy.

More of this later.

SEQUENCE 4: FLYING DIRECT FROM OUR PRESENT POSITION TO OVERHEAD THE VOR

In Sequence 2 we decided that the direct track to the VOR was 090°. We discovered this by first carrying out items 1, 2 and 3.

(1) Tune.

(2) Rotate OBS until cross pointer is centred and "TO" flag showing.

(3) Read the track against course indicator.

NOW WHAT?

(4) As the aircraft is heading 045°, and the indicated QDM is 090°, we must turn the aircraft to the right, from 045° to 090°.

FIG.14

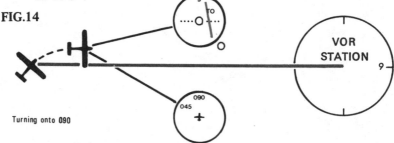

Turning onto 090

During the turn we have passed slightly north of the selected 090° track. This is why the cross-pointer is deflected to the right, indicating to the pilot that he should fly right to get back on track.

(5) Turn aircraft right, intercept heading of 105°, until cross-pointer is again in the centre, then turn back onto the track heading 090°.

FIG.15

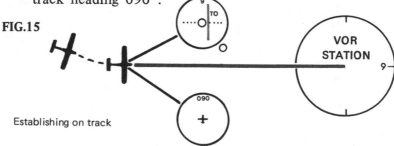

Establishing on track

(6) Maintain the selected track by flying the heading 090°, unless obeying a left or right deflection of the cross-pointer. Use common sense when deciding the number of degrees of turn needed to keep the needle centred.

10

SEQUENCE 4: GENERAL NOTE

When a VOR cross-pointer indicates turn left, or right, it is telling us that we are not on the selected track or radial, and which way we should turn to regain it. The indication must be translated by the pilot, into a sensible alteration of heading. For example, an aircraft on the right of an inbound track will be given the command to fly left. Simply turning left, and left again, and hoping for the cross-pointer to centralise, will result in the aircraft making a turn through 360° and remaining right of track.

It is up to the pilot, not simply to follow the pointer in blind and ignorant faith, but to use his head, and deduce for himself the best way to utilise the information given.

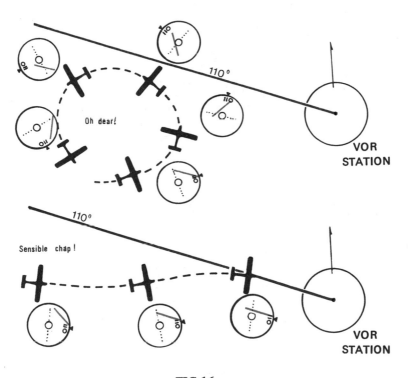

FIG.16

SEQUENCE 5: OVERHEAD THE VOR

(1) We are flying towards the station, on a track of 090°, heading 090° on the direction indicator. The VOR "TO" flag is showing, and the pointer is in the centre circle.

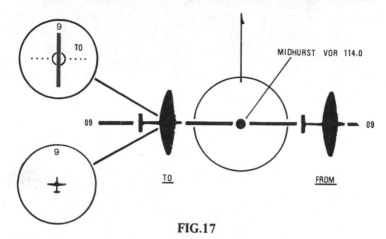

FIG.17

(2) As the aircraft nears the station, the cross-pointer will begin a deviation to the left or right. As we have already noted, the pointer livens up as we get close to the VOR. It will now indicate the smallest deviation from track or course inaccuracy. Whereas at 6 miles the width of a radial is about 600 feet, at 1 mile the radials are only 100 feet wide. So unless we are lucky enough to be dead centre on the chosen radial, we are bound to get left or right signals. If we do get a fly left signal, for instance, we should obey the cross-pointer and turn left, but as we are now very close into the station, we should restrict our changes in heading to about 10°.

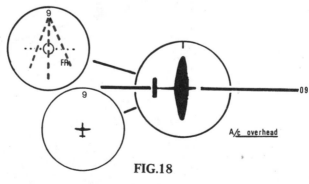

FIG.18

(3) As we pass the overhead position, we will observe the following: —

    (i)   several left/right deviations of the cross-pointer

    (ii)   the "TO" flag will disappear and the "FROM" flag will appear.

(4) We have arrived overhead the VOR. The "TO" flag may fluctuate with the "FROM" flag during station passage.

SEQUENCE 6: FLYING FROM THE VOR

(1) Having arrived overhead the VOR, we desire to continue on the same track away from the beacon.

(2) As we pass through the overhead position, we should maintain the heading of 090°, as this is the track required both "TO" and "FROM" the VOR in this particular case. Initially, the cross-pointer will waver from side to side, until the aircraft has cleared the zone of uncertainty.

(3) The "TO" flag will be replaced by the "FROM" flag.

(4) Allow the cross-pointer to settle down, then follow the demands of the cross-pointer in exactly the same way as when we were flying to the station. If the pointer gives a "fly right" demand, obey it, and turn right by 10 or 15 degrees, until the pointer is again in the middle.

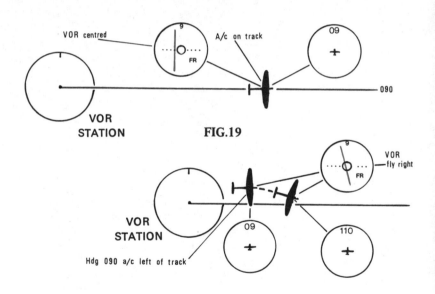

FIG.19

FIG.20

(5) We cannot fly indefinitely using the signals of one station. Range and height dictate the distance that accurate signals can be received and used. The same rules that apply to VHF communication apply to VOR. For every 1000 feet of altitude, up to about 5000 feet, 20 nms. So at 5000 feet the range is 100 nms. Above 5000 feet, ranges up to 200 miles can be received, but are unreliable beyond 120 miles.

THE MENTAL PICTURE

Whenever we use instruments and navigation aids, we must try to see a picture, in our mind's eye, of what we are doing. Staring at instruments, without translating their indications into mental pictures, can be very confusing.

Normally we use a map to orientate ourselves during the flight. A map or chart will also be available during an instrument flight, but the ground may not be visible.

The pilot, by relating the indications of his instruments to the chart on his knee, must learn to make a correctly orientated mental picture of the situation as it is now, and the way in which he wants to develop it during the next few minutes or seconds.

When using instruments and Nav aids practice translating their indications into as vivid and comprehensive a view as you possibly can. This should, eventually, become an automatic inclination.

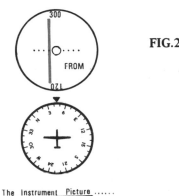

FIG.21

The Instrument Picture ......

...... The Mental Picture

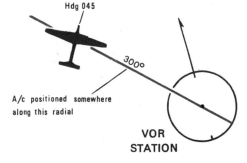

FIG.22

Hdg 045

300°

A/c positioned somewhere along this radial

VOR STATION

SEQUENCE 7: INTERCEPTING A GIVEN TRACK TO THE VOR

We come to the situation where we do not simply wish to fly direct to the VOR, but wish to intercept a particular inbound track, which is some way off from our present position.

(1) Inbound track required – 030°.

(2) Obtain the QDM of the aircraft to the VOR. Tune, Identify, turn OBS until the cross-pointer is centred and the "TO" flag is showing. Read the QDM and formulate a mental picture.

(3) If the QDM of aircraft to station is more than the track required then steer more, if less steer less.

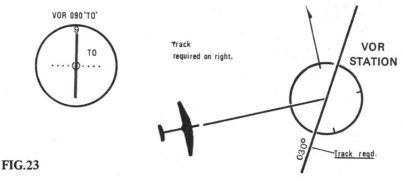

FIG.23

This rule holds good for all "TO" interceptions.

(4) In this case the QDM is 090°, as against track required of 030°, so steer more. Add about 40° to QDM of aircraft to station. 090° + 40° = 130°.

(5) Turn right onto 130°, and turn the OBS to the new required QDM of 030°. In this case the flag will read "TO" and the cross-pointer will show full deflection right.

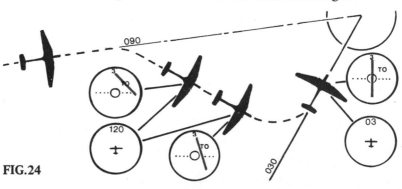

FIG.24

Notice that the VOR cross-pointer is on the right hand side of the VOR dial, and that the VOR station is on the left hand side of the aircraft.

When intercepting a QDM to a VOR station the cross-pointer will be deflected to the side of the VOR furthest away from the actual position of the VOR, until we intercept the QDM. In other words, if we set up a "TO" QDM for a VOR which lies to our left, the pointer is deflected to the right and vice versa. As we move in towards the required track our pointer leaves the edge of the dial and progresses to the centre circle. If we then turn the aircraft onto the QDM, the pointer should remain in the centre. If we simply fly through the QDM, then the pointer leaves the centre circle and continues to progress to the other side of the dial.

We can use this knowledge to determine whether or not we have gone through the required QDM without noticing it. In the example given we are still intercepting the QDM all the time the pointer is to the right of the circle. The VOR station is on our left. As soon as the pointer is to the left of the centre circle, that is on the same side as the VOR station in relation to our aircraft − then we have passed the QDM.

In the Figure 23 we can see that the pilot has decided that the QDM to the station is 090°. He then turns right, (Fig. 24) onto 120° an angle of $+90^o$, to the required QDM of 030°. This large angle of attack ensures we reach the inbound track before we reach the station's position. The heading of 120° is derived from the rule: QDM MORE, STEER MORE THAN THE QDM, TO INTERCEPT THE INBOUND TRACK. As the cross-pointer moves away from the fully deflected position, we can begin reducing the angle of interception (Fig. 25). The final stages of closing the track can best be achieved from angles of 30 to 45 degrees, so that the turn onto track does not require sudden and steep angles of bank.

(6) As the cross-pointer begins to leave the right hand side of the VOR Meter, reduce the angle of interception, turn left HDG 070°.

(7) As the cross-pointer reaches the one dot deflection, turn left again, say 045°, an angle now of only 15°.

17

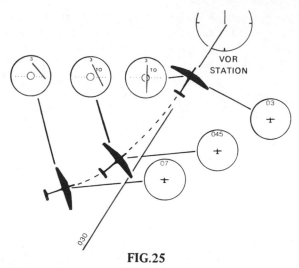

FIG.25

(8)   As the cross-pointer reaches the centre, turn onto 030°
      and obey the left/right indications of the cross-pointer.

N.B. It is only necessary to intercept the QDM by 90° or more
(as in this case) if the position of the aircraft relative to the
VOR means that there is some doubt as to the arrival of the
aircraft on the track required before it reaches the VOR (See
Fig. 26). As long as we apply the rule for intercepting we will
get the right answer every time.

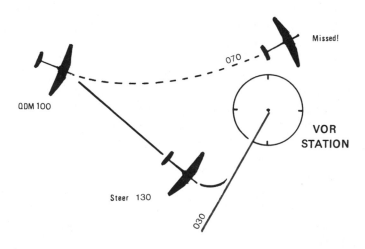

FIG.26

In most circumstances there will be ample distance and it is then possible to intercept, using the same rule — QDM more, steer more than the QDM, but the angle of interception to the required track will be less.

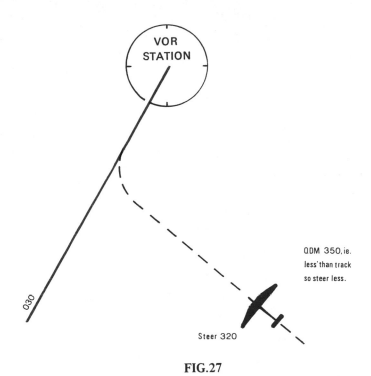

FIG.27

SEQUENCE 8: INTERCEPTING A TRACK "FROM" THE VOR

The science of flying contains certain rules which, when applied on one side of the world, work in a certain way, but on the other side of the world, work in the opposite way. Buys Ballots law is one of these, the errors of the compass are another. Working with the VOR we are faced with a similar problem. As we go from one side of the VOR to the other, the rules reverse themselves.

Sequence 7 dealt with the interception of a "TO" track in which we applied certain rules regarding the best heading to intercept the required track, and also the behaviour of the cross-pointer. The rules for the "TO" track interception were.

> Aircraft's QDM more than required QDM, steer more than the aircraft's QDM.
> Aircraft's QDM less than the required QDM, steer less than the aircraft's QDM.
> VOR station on right, cross-pointer comes in from left.
> VOR station on left, cross-pointer comes in from right.

In this sequence we have to change these rules round. The rules for the "FROM" track interception are:

> Aircraft's QDM more than required QDM, steer less than the aircraft's QDM.
> Aircraft's QDM less than required QDM, steer more than the aircraft's QDM.
> VOR on right, cross-pointer comes in from right.
> VOR on left, cross-pointer comes in from left.

In Figure 28 the following steps are being taken.
1. Ascertain the QDM which is 260°.
2. QDM 260° is more than the required track of 140°, so steer less.
3. We can see that a sensible heading to bring us onto this track is about 220°.
4. Turn the aircraft onto the new heading of 220°, and turn the OBS on your VOR so that the required track of 140° is set. Note that with the station on the right of the aircraft, the cross-pointer is deflected to the right when the "FROM" track is set.
5. As the aircraft nears the track, the cross-pointer will start to move towards the centre. When this happens the

20

pilot will commence turning left and reducing his angle of interception ready for a smooth turn onto track.

6. On track, the pointer will be in the middle and the flag will indicate "FROM".

7. In stage 4 the pilot sets up the required track, on the VOR. This track of 140° is nearly 90° away from our present radial of 080°. In these circumstances the VOR will not immediately give any satisfactory readings until the aircraft reaches a point less than 70 to 75 degrees from the 140° radial. The "off" flag may show, and the pointer waver around, until we leave this area of ambiguous uncertainty. (See Fig. 28).

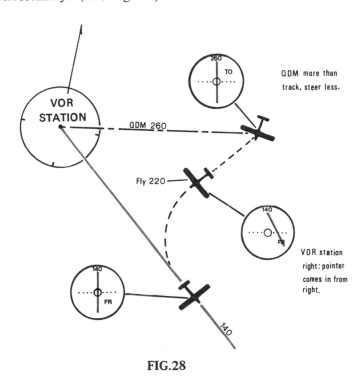

FIG.28

SEQUENCE 9: CHANGING TRACK AFTER PASSING OVER-HEAD THE VOR

Having passed the VOR we wish to change our track and fly from the VOR on a new radial.

1. We arrive overhead the station on a track of 325°.
2. The flag changes to "FROM". The new track required is 252°.
3. This new track lies to our left, so turn left. The heading is a matter of common sense. About 220° or even 200° for a quicker interception.
4. Select the 252° radial on the VOR and as the cross-pointer leaves the fully deflected position, bring the aircraft gradually onto track.

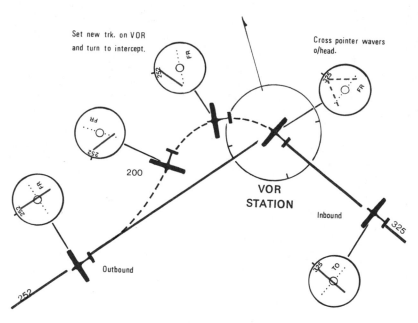

FIG.29

SECTION TWO

OUR ENEMY, THE WIND

SEQUENCE 1: (6/7/8 FROM FIRST SECTION)

Flying to the VOR
Overhead the VOR
Flying from the VOR

GENERAL NOTE

How does the wind affect us? In exactly the same way as it would on any cross country flight. It slows us down, or speeds us up: drifts us left, or drifts us right, or any combination of these possibilities. It is generally a damn nuisance, but we learn to live with it, and use it if we can, to our advantage.

The first thing to get quite straight in our heads, is the absolute necessity of acquiring as much pre-flight information as possible. "Beacon hopping" can be dangerous, unless backed up by a grasp of the equipment, and a knowledge of the weather details. Don't admire those, who, when asked how they intend making it, in the apparently foul conditions, reply, "just tune in the VOR's, old boy." A cross-pointer behaving in an "odd" way, or what seems to us odd, because we are not sure where the wind is coming from, can lead us to suspect our equipment. We alternate between belief and disbelief which soon causes a certain amount of cerebral confusion. If we suspect our VOR for the right reasons, this is fine, as we can take a positive course of corrective action. But blaming the VOR, when in fact its information is good, leads to incorrect corrections, so get yourself properly clued up before take-off. It's nice to know if we will experience 40 kts of tail wind, head wind, or cross wind, during our flight.

FIG.30

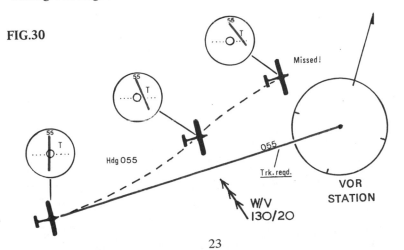

23

In Figure 30 we have a familiar situation.
Track required 055° (M)
W/V 130/20
TAS 120 kts

The mental picture looks something like this.
Tracking 055° (M)
But wind is 75° on the starboard side
Drift is probably about 10° and G/S is
about the same as the TAS 120

You can put the numbers on the Navigation Computer to arrive at the correct answer.

It is obvious that we should be steering at least 10° more than 055° (M) to maintain the track.

The VOR gives its own picture
Aircraft on track pointer centred
Direction indicator shows heading 055° (M)
Aircraft drifted to left of track pointer shows a steer right indication
Turn aircraft to right, heading about 100°
Don't forget we have to stop the drift and regain the track
As the VOR cross-pointer reaches the centre turn the aircraft back onto a heading to allow for drift and maintain the track.
The final picture should be cross pointer in centre
Heading 065° (+ or − a few degrees)

FIG.31

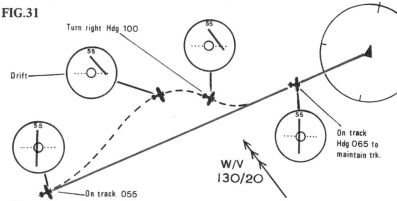

We now have the advantage of a continuous indication of our track keeping, from the VOR. If the wind is not exactly as forecast, or substantially changes its speed and direction, the VOR pointer will again show us to which side we have strayed from track, and which way to go to regain it. Having regained it, it may be that we have allowed too much or too little for drift. In which case, fly back to the track, and offset a recalculated amount of drift.

Use the strength and direction of the wind intelligently.

1. If the wind is strong, and at 90° to your track, and you are on the downwind side of the track to boot, use large angles of 40 to 60 degrees, to regain the track. Always err into the wind, as it is far easier to correct upwind errors, than downwind errors. If we find ourselves too far upwind, we can use the wind to help us, but if we are downwind of the required track, it's a struggle all the way.

2. When on the upwind side of the track, you can regain it by using smaller angles than before, but this time, remember, that as soon as we approach the track, we must anticipate the turn onto it, and get the aircraft heading back into the wind, to stop us going right through the track. We can take advantage of the cross pointer by watching its rate of movement across the dial, and judging from this the "lead" required and rate of turn suitable to achieve the track.

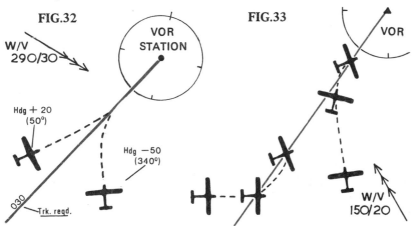

FIG.32   VOR STATION   **FIG.33**   VOR

W/V 290/30

Hdg + 20 (50°)

Hdg —50 (340°)

030   Trk. reqd.

W/V 150/20

DIFFERENT SOLUTIONS FOR DIFFERENT SITUATIONS

(a) This pilot comes up to the track at a large angle and turns onto the heading required to maintain it, only when he has actually reached it. It would do no harm to overshoot the track slightly.

(b) He must start the turn early and come back across the track and into wind.

SEQUENCE 2: (9/ FROM FIRST SECTION)

The wind has no other effects on the problems of track interception apart from those already mentioned. In the examples below, most of the previous exercises are covered, and a few more besides.

1.   To intercept 360° from VOR A.

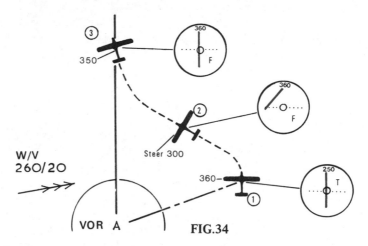

FIG.34

(a)   Aircraft obtains QDM of 250°.
(b)   Aircraft turns onto 300° (QDM LESS, STEER MORE) sets VOR Radial 360° – pointer shows deflection left.
(c)   Aircraft on track 360°, heading is 350° to allow for wind.

2.   To leave above track on QDM 270° towards VOR B.

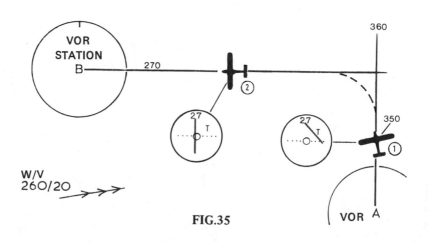

FIG.35

(a) Aircraft tunes to VOR B and sets QDM 270° on dial. Pointer shows fly right.

(b) Pointer comes in from side furthest from VOR.

(c) Aircraft established on 270°, no drift.

3. To recalculate Drift. G/S and W/V.

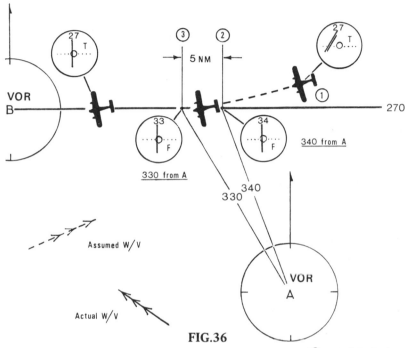

FIG.36

(a) The pilot of an aircraft has been flying 270° to VOR B, but notices a fly left signal from the cross-pointer. He turns onto 240° and regains track, keeping it by steering 260°. Alert as ever, the pilot decides that the wind is further round to his port side, and that his ground speed is greater than previously calculated. He can, by using VOR B, and VOR A, do three things. Find his position, find his ground speed and find the W/V.

(b) POSITION: As the pilot knows that he is tracking 270° towards B, he can, by tuning a radial from A, get a cross bearing, which will give him a reasonable fix. The accuracy of this fix depends on distance, angle between track and VOR, and height, not to mention the errors of the equipment. However, under the right circumstances it is sensible **to assume that the fix is reasonably accurate for position** finding.

27

(c) G/S AND W/V: If he takes another position line from VOR A, after a recorded time interval and having marked the last fix on the map, he can measure the distance travelled between Position A and Position B.

1. Time between each fix − 2 minutes
2. Distance covered 5 nautical miles
3. G/S = 150 knots
4. Heading 260° to make good track of 270° so drift is 10° stbd.
5. It looks as if the wind has backed to South east. Put the information onto the computer.
    W/V 125/38.

Tips, Pitfalls and Checks

1. Is the frequency correct?
2. Is the ident. correct?
3. Has the VOR frequency been changed?
4. Is the VOR on the air or has it been switched off for service? The stations are switched off once every 28 days for maintenance. These times can be found in the Air Pilot or Aerad Flight Guide.
5. Are the flags giving the "on" signals required?
6. Have you got the "to" track selected, when you want the "from" radial, or the other way round?
7. Are you too low, or too far away, to receive good signals from the station you require?
8. When using two VOR meters in your aircraft, each tuned to a separate station, are you looking at the right one? or have you got them all muddled up? Ensure that you use constant vigilance over this.
9. Have you selected 030° instead of 300°, or 120° instead of 210°?
10. Has the "to" flag been replaced by the "from" flag while you were looking the other way?
11. When approaching the VOR station, don't forget other people may be doing the same thing. They, like you, are probably cruising cheerfully at 2000 feet. LOOKOUT. And again please. LOOKOUT. Use the radio where possible to get appropriate information on any conflicting traffic.
12. Is the DI synchronised with the compass?

13. Are you trying to make a home-made let down into Aunty Vi's back garden, in order to impress the dear lady before she signs her will. If you are, then Aunty will be more than interested in the contents of your own last testament.

14. Remember that any equipment of a mechanical or electrical nature is almost bound to malfunction at some time, and may do so at an inconvenient moment, so do not put all thy trust in these ungodly things.

Checks

1. Before entering an aircraft, ensure that the aerials are in good condition, not bent or broken.

2. Before switching on the master switch, check that all radio equipment including the VOR, is switched off.

3. After engine checks are complete, selected frequency and turn on set.

4. If you are at an aerodrome with its very own VOR, or if it is possible to receive a good signal from your ground position, then these checks can be carried out during the pre-flight checks. In most circumstances you will have to wait until airbourne.

5. Identify the call sign.

6. Turn the OBS until the cross pointer is centred and the flag reads "to" or "from". Then ensure that the "off" flag has disappeared.

7. Check that the QDM, or QDR, whichever is set, looks sensible, and agrees with your own calculations.

8. Turn the OBS bearing scale through 360°, and watch the behaviour of the cross-pointer, and the to/from flags. The cross-pointer should pass the central position twice and the to/from flags appear once each.

9. When tuning any VOR
   Check ident
   Check QDM/QDR
   Check off flag gone
   Check cross-pointer deflections
   Check the to/from flags for correct indications

10. Some VOR equipment can be pointer checked by simply pressing a small button on the OBS TURN knob.

THE LOCALISER NEEDLE

It is not a part of this book to explain, or teach, the ILS, Instrument Landing System, but as many VOR installations allow for the cross-pointer to be tuned to a localiser, we should know how to make limited use of it. The localiser is that part of the ILS which indicates Runway centre line information to the pilot. By selecting frequencies between 108 and 112 Mcs, and providing your set has a receiving capability for the localiser, the cross-pointer is converted to localiser.

Characteristics of the Localiser, compared to VOR

1. With the localiser switched on, the OBS is redundant. The localiser responds to runway centre line, or left/right signals to the selected runway only.
2. The to/from flags are likewise invalid and will indicate 'off'.
3. The localiser needle gives useful information under the following circumstances:—
(A) When the aircraft is less than 30° either side of the runway centre line.
(B) When the aircraft is less than 30 miles out from the threshold — although they can, depending on height, be used at greater distance — their accuracy is unchecked.

The sensitivity of the localiser needle is four times that of the VOR cross pointer. This means that each dot is equal to ½° and full deflection is equal to only 2½°.

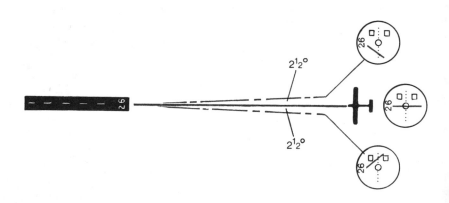

FIG.37

USES OF THE LOCALISER NEEDLE

1. To acquire a position line when crossing an ILS extended centre line.

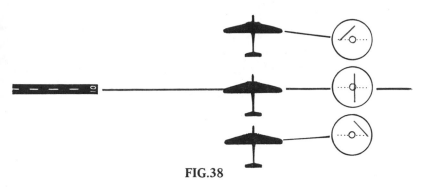

FIG.38

2. To home towards a threshold from a position along the extended centre line.

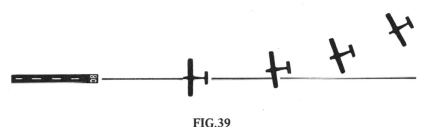

FIG.39

3. To use it in conjunction with Glide slope and execute a precision approach.
   As we are not dealing with full ILS here, we will leave this one out.

4. To home on a centre line and descend to a specified height, from which a landing can be made providing the runway is visible.

In this type of approach, no glide slope information is available, but with the assistance of ground control, and/or other NAV aids, an approach can be made, subject to certain limitations, which will be governed by your own experience, and the published minima of the let down pattern. We shall assume, for the purposes of the next exercise, that the pilot has permission to make an approach to an aerodrome, where the visibility is 3000 metres in rain, below a cloud base of 1000 feet.

The first problem is to put the aircraft onto the centre line and this is generally accomplished by using another aid, plus assistance from a Radar controller.

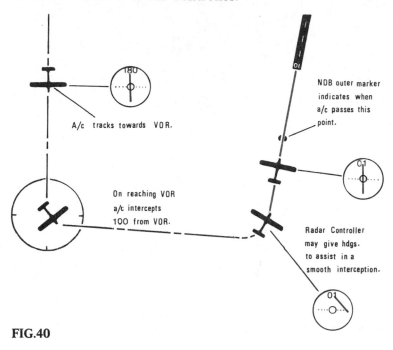

FIG.40

1. The aircraft is cleared to the VOR.
2. On reaching the VOR, it turns left to make good the track of $100°$ from the VOR.
3. The aim is to position the aircraft on 'finals' at a distance of about 6 miles.
4. If Radar is available, the controller will assist you by giving headings to intercept the centre line.
5. Anticipation of wind effect is of prime importance as you are following a very narrow band of airspace indeed. The best way to make a proper job of it, is to get the runway heading firmly in your mind and if there is a 'bug' on the DI, bug it.

   Turn onto this heading +/− drift. Then if you get a fly left or right signal, turn in the direction indicated by no more than 10° at a time. Less is better if you can anticipate the drift and keep it all within narrow limits. Whichever way you turn, keep the runway heading in your mind as the datum upon which all your turns are based.

6. The aircraft is now tracking down the extended centre line at a distance of about 5 miles, and at a height of about 1600 feet. The final descent can now commence to the minimum descent altitude.

This is accomplished by an initial descent to about 1300 feet, followed by level flight until the 'marker' is crossed. The marker will be either an ADF beacon, known as a locator beacon, or a straightforward marker. Both are referred to, in this context, as the Outer Marker.

The ADF marker is a Radio Beacon, which indicates that the aircraft has crossed overhead by a reversal of the indicator needle.

The 75 mc marker does the same thing by triggering the blue marker light in the cockpit, providing the aircraft has one.

The marker is situated about 4 miles out from the threshold and once the aircraft has crossed it, at the correct height, the aircraft can recommence its descent to the minimum height, at which it will fly level until it sees the field, or overshoots. The stop watch should be started as the aircraft crosses the outer marker and the time from outer marker to threshold noted from the chart. This time varies with the ground speed.

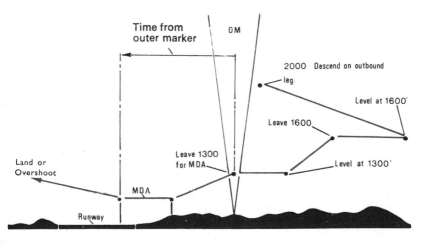

FIG.41

33

THE VOR APPROACH PATTERN

The ultimate aim of the pilot and his navigation aid, is to use it to make a descent to an aerodrome in dirty weather. This is done by following clearly defined and specified tracks in azimuth, and conforming to a particular height profile, which while keeping the aircraft away from disaster, will at the same time allow it to descend to an airfield beneath a low cloud ceiling, and from thence to a visual landing.

Included in this chapter is an example of a VOR approach 'plate'. This is produced by International Aeradio and is a legally recognised representation of the let down pattern for the VOR on runway 27 at Guernsey. The charts are amended from time to time, and as soon as a new one is issued the previous one becomes officially out of date.

Study it carefully and absorb the relevant information. Any pilot should make a study in detail and in advance of the flight, of all the salient points relating to this critical manoeuvre.

1.   Look at the chart and orientate your mental picture to that of the actual direction from which your aircraft will enter the area, and approach the pattern. By doing this you will be able to assess the first moves to make on arrival over the beacon.

2.   Note the safety height for the area, and the height from which the descent will commence.

3.   Study the azimuth plan or track plan, and note the various headings. Pencil in any that are not marked but that you think you may need. For example it is advisable to insert the still air heading for the procedure turn.

4.   Study the descent, or profile pattern, getting certain facts firmly in your mind. Altitude at each stage, minimum descent altitude, and OCL (Obstacle Clearance Limit). This is the height below which the aircraft must not descend without visual contact with the runway. A private pilot must work out his own MDA, but in any case it should not be less than the OCL. Private pilots should note that all professional approaches are carried out to safety minimum for cloud base and horizontal visibility. No minimums are issued to private individuals and this is a great pity. Minimum descent altitude should be not less than the OCL rounded up to the nearest 50' and plussed up to the next multiple of 100.

$$OCL\ 260 = 300 + 100 = 400\ feet$$

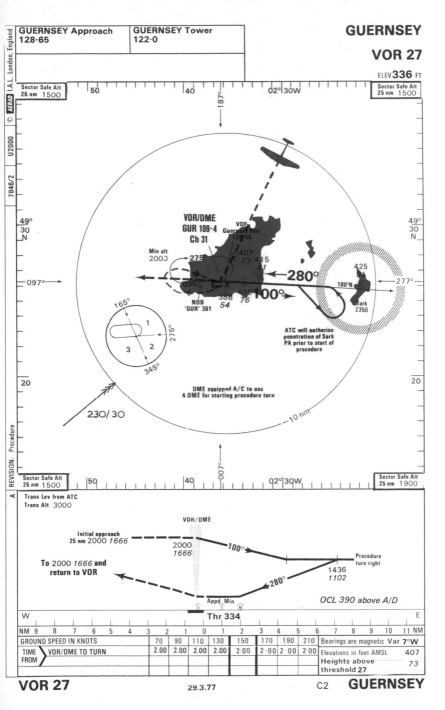

GUERNSEY Approach
128·65

GUERNSEY Tower
122·0

ELEV **336** FT

I.A.L. London, England
U2000 © IBAD
7846/2
REVISION: Procedure
A

Sector Safe Alt
25 nm 1500

Sector Safe Alt
25 nm 1500

Sector Safe Alt
25 nm 1500

Sector Safe Alt
25 nm 1900

50   40   02°30W

187°

49°30N

49°30N

097°

277°

VOR/DME
GUR 109·4
Ch 31

VDF
Guernsey Twr
128·65

Min alt
2000   275°

407
73 415
61

280°

425

100°R

100°

096°

419
76

388
54

NDB
'GUR' 361

Sark
2350

165°

1
3   2

275°

345°

ATC will authorise
penetration of Sark
PA prior to start of
procedure

230/30

DME equipped A/C to use
4 DME for starting procedure turn

—10 nm

20   20

50   40   02°30W

007°

Trans Lev from ATC
Trans Alt 3000

VOR/DME

Initial approach
25 nm 2000 *1666*

2000
1666

100°

2000
1666

Procedure
turn right

To 2000 *1666* and
return to VOR

1436
1102

280°

OCL 390 above A/D

Appd_Min

Thr 334

W   E

NM 9	8	7	6	5	4	3	2	1	0	1	2	3	4	5	6	7	8	9	10	11 NM

GROUND SPEED IN KNOTS	70	90	110	130	150	170	190	210
TIME FROM VOR/DME TO TURN	2.00	2.00	2.00	2.00	2.00	2.00	2.00	2.00

Bearings are magnetic Var 7°W

Elevations in feet AMSL   407
Heights above threshold 27   *73*

VOR 27   29.3.77   C2   GUERNSEY

Visibility should not be less than 1500 metres.
Greater if the airfield is not equipped with approach lights.
How does the inexperienced private pilot avoid trying to
attempt landings below these minimums. He should stay
on the ground ,if there is any doubt at all about the
conditions being worse than his capabilities will allow for
a safe flight.
Always underestimate your abilities when it comes to
pilot versus weather.

5.   Make sure you know the overshoot procedure, so that in
the event of the runway remaining invisible at the correct
time and height, you will not hesitate to commence the
overshoot.

**The approach and overshoot is divided into the following
segments:**

1.   The en route approach to the beacon.
2.   The hold, if required.
3.   The achievement of the outbound track.
4.   The procedure turn.
5.   Final approach.
6.   The landing
          or
     The overshoot.

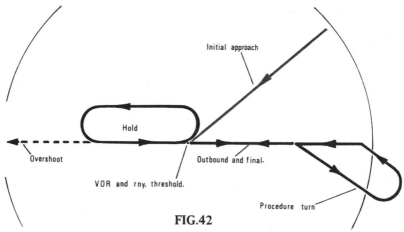

Initial approach

Hold

Overshoot

Outbound and final.

VOR and rny. threshold.

Procedure turn

FIG.42

Most VOR let down procedures are associated with a beacon
placed adjacent to the threshold, but there are many variations
to the let down theme and you must realise that each one has
its own peculiarities.

THE CHART

Guernsey – runway 27 VOR frequency 109.4
Top left – communications frequencies
In each corner – min. safe altitude.
Top right – airfield elevation.
Plan of pattern.
Holding pattern with inbound and outbound headings.
Frequencies of the facilities.
Outbound track, procedure turn and final track.
The overshoot.
The profile box includes the OCL–390, which should be rounded up to 450.
You will also find a series of times against ground speed.
In this case 2 minutes is specified for the time outbound, Thus in still air the timing from threshold VOR out on the procedure and back to the threshold would be:–

    2 minutes (from beacon)
    1 minute (procedure turn outbound)
    1 minute (turn)
    ½ minute (back to inbound track)
    ½ minute (to reach place where turn commenced)
    and 2 minutes (to the beacon)

Total: 7 minutes.
The timing is altered by a wind component because the outbound leg and inbound leg will be flown at different ground speeds.

THE HOLD:

    The hold is a way of bringing an aircraft to a particular position, and then keeping it in a specified area and returning it to the beacon once every four minutes. The aircraft may commence its descent in the hold or may simply be asked to waste time until it is clear for it to commence its approach.

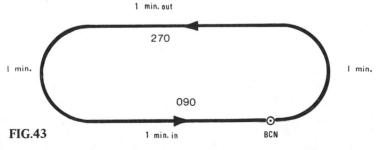

FIG.43

It looks like a racetrack and is sometimes called a racetrack. Including the turns the hold is four minutes in duration.

There are three problems connected with the hold:—

Entry
Drift
Timing

ENTRY:

The approach to the holding pattern is divided into three sectors, each section requiring a different entry procedure.

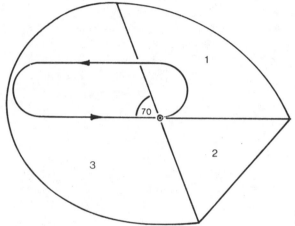

FIG.44

Starting with Sector Three: DIRECT ENTRY

The aircraft flies to overhead the beacon and then as soon as it is overhead it enters the hold direct, by turning onto the outbound track. Rates of turn are rate 1 or 3° per second.

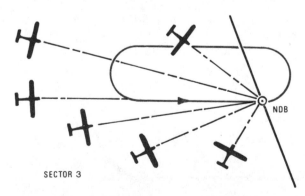

SECTOR 3

FIG.45

38

Sector Two: TEAR DROP or OFFSET

The aircraft comes up to the holding beacon, and then, after passing overhead the beacon, turns towards the outbound track at an interception angle of 30°.

A Sector 2 at Guernsey would mean that after passing overhead the beacon the aircraft turns onto a heading of 305° + or − the drift, and then after one minute, turns back to the beacon on the inbound track.

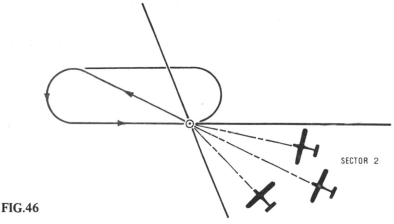

SECTOR 2

FIG.46

Sector One: PARALLEL ENTRY

The aircraft flies up to the beacon, and as it passes overhead, it turns onto the outbound heading. This will cause it to track away from the beacon, but on the inbound side of the hold. After one minute + or − an allowance for wind, the aircraft in this case turns right, and back through the pattern to the beacon. The aim is to put the aircraft on the inbound QDM before reaching the beacon.

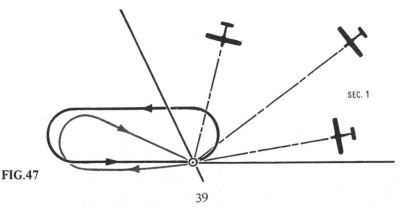

SEC. 1

FIG.47

Drift and timing during the entry to the hold should be allowed for, by keeping the aircraft into the wind to correct for the drift on the joining legs. Timing can be controlled by allowing one second for every knot of head wind or tail wind component, adding or subtracting as necessary.

Obviously holds are varied in orientation and headings so here are a few of them:–

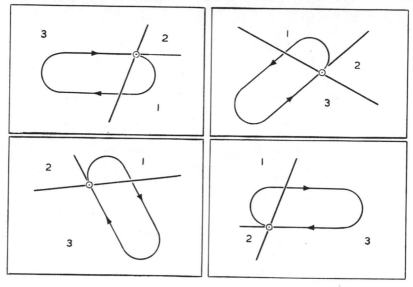

FIG.48

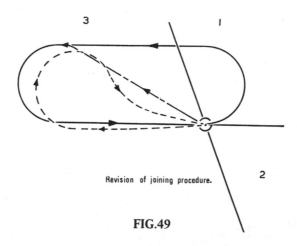

Revision of joining procedure.

FIG.49

DRIFT IN THE HOLD

During the hold the wind affects drift and timing.
1. As the aircraft makes the first turn.
2. On the outbound leg.
3. On the inbound turn.
4. On the inbound leg.

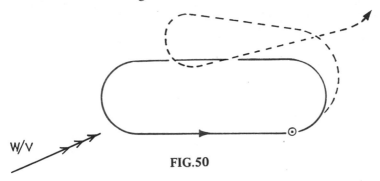

FIG.50

DRIFT: We counteract the drift on the turns during the outbound leg and as we also allow for the drift of the leg itself, we have to apply three times the drift on the outbound leg.

TIME: Allow one second for every knot of tail wind or head wind component. Add for head wind: Subtract for tail wind.

If the true airspeed is 120 kts and the W/V is 230/30 the Guernsey hold will produce 10° of drift and 20 kts of headwind component on the outbound leg.

The timing starts as we pass over the beacon. As we want to add about 20 seconds to the outbound leg, the time from the beacon to the inbound turn is 2.20 seconds. 1 minute for the turn outbound and 1 minute 20 seconds for the outbound leg. The drift is 10° to starboard. Three times 10° is 30°, so the heading on the outboard leg is 275 − 30 = 245°.

The hold will now look something like this, Fig. 51 and although the pattern has become distorted, the end product is to put the aircraft back on the inbound track.

Obviously, in very strong winds holding can become difficult. In conditions of strong winds needing more than 45° of drift allowance, it becomes improbable that you will be able to achieve a perfect holding pattern.

41

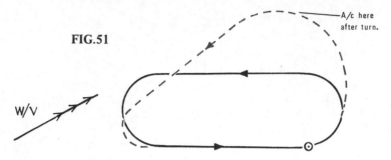

FIG.51

W/V

REASONS FOR HOLDING

Holds are usually required in bad weather, when a large number of aircraft arrive at the same airport at the same time. The worse the weather the longer the hold is likely to be.

There are other reasons, such as delays on the runway itself. Whatever the reason, holding patterns are designed to keep you in the specified area, at a safe height, until the delay is over.

Summary of hold:
1.   Entry.
2.   Allowance for drift.
3.   Allowance for time.
4.   Regaining the inbound QDM.
5.   Try and keep' the time on each circuit within the time segment.   3 mins 40 secs to 4 mins 20 secs.

During a holding pattern, close attention must be paid to altitude in turns, co-ordinated and smooth handling, and an accurate note taken of any Air Traffic Control instructions, with particular attention to altimeter settings and altitude.

During entry to the hold allow single drift.

The indications of the VOR during the hold will be as shown below:—

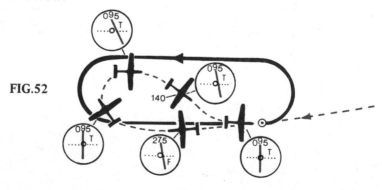

FIG.52

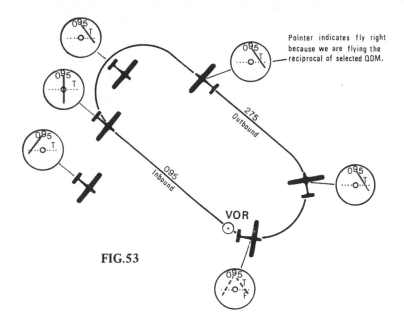

Pointer indicates fly right because we are flying the reciprocal of selected QDM.

275 Outbound

095 Inbound

VOR

FIG.53

THE PROCEDURE TURN

After flying the outbound track (which happens to be the reverse of the inbound track,) we want to "Turn again Whittington" and change course 180° to fly the same track in the opposite direction. One way to do this is to make a procedure turn. This is accomplished by turning 45°, right or left, as specified, holding the new heading for about 1 minute, and then turning through 180°, so that you intercept the final track at an angle of 45°. In fact we hope to make a continuous turn through 225° and find ourselves on the inbound track.

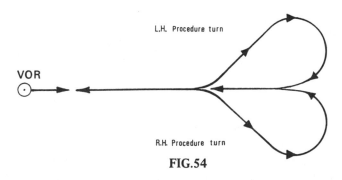

L.H. Procedure turn

VOR

R.H. Procedure turn

FIG.54

43

DRIFT

Again the correct allowance for drift and timing are important so that the aircraft is in the right place after the turn inbound.   Allow   for   drift   on the first leg of the procedure and   one   second   for   every   knot   of   head   wind or tail   wind component. Reduce the outbound time with tail wind, and increase with head wind.

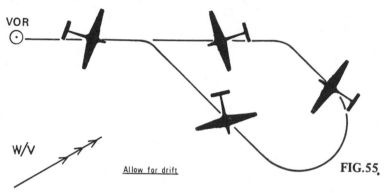

Allow for drift

FIG.55

We are tracking 095° and we know that we start the procedure turn after flying this track for 2 minutes.   We then start the stop watch and turn onto the 1 minute procedure turn. If we were heading 105° on the outbound track of 095° before the turn, then we turn right +45° to a heading of 150°.

THE VOR DESCENT AND APPROACH

1. As we approach the airport from the NE, level at 2000 feet QNH, we call up the Guernsey approach controller. The call will be made when the Jersey zone radar unit releases us to the Guernsey frequency. It is very important to copy down the airfield data given to you by the controller, especially the QNH and QFE. The QFE must be set on the altimeter before commencing the approach.

2. Tune and identify the VOR.

3. Set the QDM and maintain this to the station.

4. During the tracking inbound assess the effect of wind on the various legs of the pattern. Commit as much as possible of the major pattern features to memory. Decide on the type of entry to the hold or the best way to enter the descent pattern if there is no hold required.

5. Knowing the wind to be 230/30 we can decide on the approximate headings and timings.

We note that a Sector One type entry to the hold will be required and that even if no hold is required this is still the best method to enter the pattern.

6. The altitude at the VOR for the first turn is 2000 feet.
7. On reaching the VOR: (a) start the stopwatch
    (b) turn onto $275^{\circ} -15^{\circ} = 260^{\circ}$
    (c) call overhead beacon.
8. Set the VOR Bearing to 100° as this is the QDR of the first track.
9. Fly 260° for 1 minute 20 seconds.
10. When time is up, turn right onto a heading of about 150°. This will enable us to reach the inbound track before passing the VOR. The cross pointer can now be obeyed to gain the track.

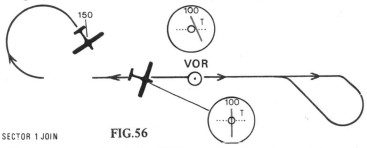

SECTOR 1 JOIN   **FIG.56**

11. When next overhead the VOR, restart the stopwatch, maintain the QDR 100° from the VOR and call "Outbound". Fly the outbound leg for 2 minutes to allow for the time given in the G/S time box in the bottom section of the let down chart. The heading required to maintain the track will be about 110°.
    During the outbound leg we descend to 1100 on the QFE. Remember to set the QFE on number one altimeter, and QNH on number two if you have it.
12. At the end of the two minutes, the procedure turn should be initiated by a right turn onto $110 + 45 = 155^{\circ}$. At the end of the full minute, in this case turn left onto 325 (the reciprocal of 145) $- 10^{\circ}$ for drift allowance. Whilst on the procedure turn, remember to reset the final QDM bearing on the VOR, 280°. The flag should now read 'to' and the pointer shows fly right. As you come round onto 135°, watch and follow the demands of the pointer. As soon as it starts to move into the centre, turn onto the inbound heading of 280°. Use the cross pointer to maintain

45

the track, which, in this case will require you to steer 270°
to stay on track. If the pointer moves from right to left
before you have completed the turn onto finals, this means
that the aircraft was not flown for sufficient time on the
procedure outbound and is now north of track. In that
case, keep turning onto about 255° to get the pointer
back in the centre.

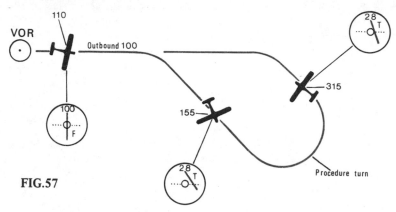

FIG.57

13. As soon as the aircraft is established on the final track,
     commence descent to 450 feet and level off. Continue
     inbound at 450 feet until the airfield is in sight. The timing
     from the completion of the turn to threshold is not required
     on this approach as the VOR is located on the airfield.
     However, the time will be about 3 minutes 35 seconds and
     it is a good idea to use this knowledge as an additional
     aid on finals.

During the whole procedure, it must be borne in mind that
all the manoeuvres take place very close into the station so the
cross pointer will be lively throughout.

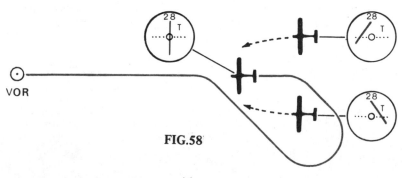

FIG.58

The ADF

EXPLANATION OF DIAGRAM LAYOUT:
Each figure contains the following information:-

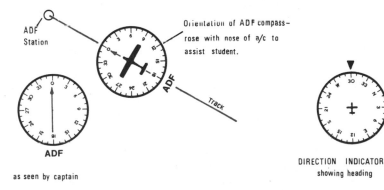

FIG.59

GENERAL

The ADF is known, like many things in aviation, by several alternative names. Automatic Direction Finding, Non Directional Beacon and Radio Compass. In fact, these terms can be classified as being component parts of the same system.

ADF (Automatic Direction Finding) is the overall name given to the whole system.

NDB (Non Directional Beacon) is the term given to the ground equipment.

RADIO COMPASS is the name given to the airborne indicator.

But the correct name of this is a Relative Bearing Indicator.

FIG.60

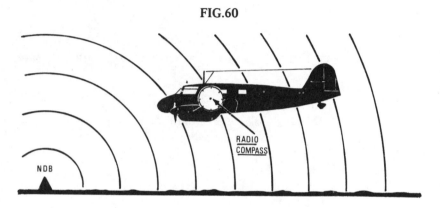

Although you would not see many references to the VOR before 1960, you will find ADF in abundance, right back to the aeronautical ark. In one form or another it is the grand old lady of radio navigation. The modern ADF is simply an improved version of the old system whereby pilots sat, trailing aerials, and turning loops around above their heads, and repeating everything twice on the radio.

"Hallo Croydon, Hallo Croydon, this is George Able Baker Charlie Dog, George Able Baker Charlie Dog. Are you receiving me? Are you receiving me? Hallo Croydon, over."

The answer was usually a slight increase in the static, followed by the faintest of voices carried as if it were whispered into the very teeth of a howling gale. But these barely audible and disjointed sounds would cause the navigator to grin excitedly, and leaning amorously close to the Captain, give him the thumbs up sign for field in sight. Then both would look down over the side, their goggles misted, their scarves of white silk streaming behind.

"Got it?"

"No."

"There, down there, just ahead of the road."

"I've got it, here we go then."

All was calm again on the aeroplane as it glided down to its landfall.

The basic concept of the Radio Compass is that a Pointer on the pilot's instrument points at the station, and thus shows the relationship of the aircraft's "O", or nose position, to this station. This relationship is known as the Relative Bearing.

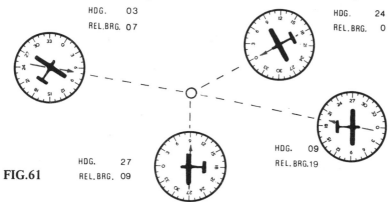

FIG.61

Regardless of the aircraft's heading, the pointer still shows the relative bearing. The VOR pointer is in the centre providing the aircraft is on the selected track, but irrespective of the heading. The ADF pointer is centred or zeroed, only when the station is dead ahead.

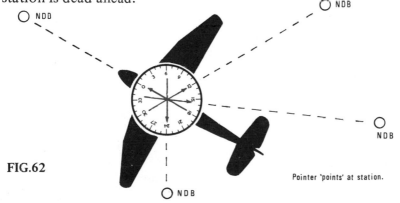

FIG.62

Pointer 'points' at station.

Thus the foundation of this aid is that it gives continuous information regarding the direction of a station and can therefore be used as a Homer, Fix, Bearing or Let Down Aid.

All the exercises in this book are demonstrated on a fixed compass rose, round which the pointer rotates to show the relative bearing. The alternative to this is a rotating compass card. This system is called Radio Magnetic Indicator or RMI. The RMI gives the actual magnetic bearing and is, in fact, an ADF combined with a Direction Indicator, but as few light aircraft are equipped with an RMI we shall concentrate on the first type.

THE GROUND STATION

The ground station consists of a transmitter and aerial system which operates on a chosen frequency between 200 and 800 Kcs or Khz. This is the low and medium frequency band. The power of the transmitter is varied according to the range required. Airway beacons being useable at around 100 miles, and airfield locator beacons around 10/20 miles.

The signals put out by the transmitter will follow the earth's curve so that the range is not restricted by line of sight and, in fact, can be satisfactorily received at ground level.

The signals deteriorate in strength with increasing distance from the beacon, and this is caused by the electrical resistance of the surface over which the signal is travelling. Greater ranges and accuracy should be obtained over water than over deserts for instance.

If the intervening terrain, is particularly fierce, such as the Alps or Pyrenees, it will tend to distort the signal so that the indicated bearings are suspect due to bending of the wave.

The time of day or night is also a factor affecting the accuracy of the incoming signal. Due to the changes that take place in the height of the reflecting layer above the earth, and the electron activity within it, uniform reception over the twenty four hours is not achieved. Day time is best, although even here reception will be affected by periodic Solar activity. At sunrise and sunset and during the night, range and accuracy are reduced. One reason for this is that at night some sky waves will mix it with the ground waves. The sky wave will strike the aerial at a different angle and cause an inaccurate bearing — there will also be some interference from other stations. Sunrise and Sunset are the periods when greatest changes are taking place in the electrical activity of the reflecting layer.

ADF equipment must always be used with a certain amount of circumspection, and it must be realised that the pointer does not just lock on, and get you there without further aggravation. The equipment can be difficult to tune, and the pointer tends to wander about a bit. A summary of the defects will be found at the end of the book.

The ground station also transmits a three letter morse identification signal. Most stations carry the morse ident signal by modulating the continuous transmission of the fixed signal, and thus it can be heard by turning up the volume of the Radio Compass. Some stations, however, transmit an inaudible signal.

For this ident to be heard, it must be processed at the receiver, i.e. the aircraft, and given a tone by introducing a separately keyed signal on a slightly different frequency, which alternates or beats against the signal transmitted, and this produces an audible sound. The name of the receiver equipment to make this signal audible is the Beat Frequency Oscillator, or BFO.

THE AIRCRAFT EQUIPMENT:

The Non Directional Beacon is transmitting a signal which must be received, identified and interpreted by the aircraft receiver. The airborne equipment is required to carry out the following functions.

Tune

Identify and test

To find the direction of the incoming signal

To transmit this information to the pilot's instrument

To give the pilot a pictorial display of this information

The aircraft end of the ADF consists of two aerials, a wireless receiver set, and a relative bearing indicator. (Radio Compass).

The two aerials, sense and loop, are used in conjunction to find the direction of the signal and resolve the question of whether the signal is in front or behind. The loop rotates until it receives the lowest signal strength in the aerial, and this is called the 'null' position.

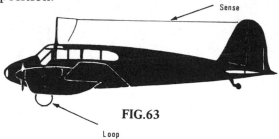

Sense

Loop

FIG.63

The sense aerial compensates, and resolves the ambiguity, by causing a stronger signal from the beacon side of the loop. The sense aerial is also the receiving aerial for the audible signals of the wireless set.

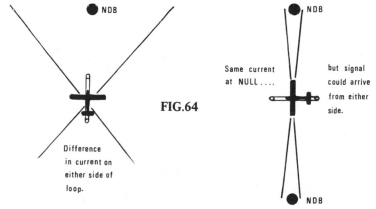

NDB

NDB

Same current at NULL....

but signal could arrive from either side.

FIG.64

Difference in current on either side of loop.

NDB

THE SET

The mind boggles when confronted with the huge variety of sets, all attempting to achieve the same thing, but there have been vast improvements in their construction and operation over the years. The cardinal development as far as the pilot is concerned is the greater ease of selecting and tuning the frequency on ADF's manufactured after 1970. Instead of the old and rather confusing wireless tuning dial, which is likely to drive a pilot insane in turbulent conditions, we now have the digital tuner which, in fact, works in exactly the same way as the VHF tuner mechanism.

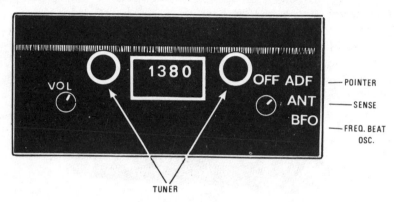

TO TUNE THE SET·

1. Select the required frequency and frequency band
2. Select 'ANT', or sense aerial. This presents the strongest ident signal.
3. Switch on the set
4. Turn up the volume
5. Listen for the correct ident. If the station is AI, that is,, requires the BFO to make the ident audible, then turn from ANT to BFO or CW.
6 The station is fine tuned by obtaining the strongest ident signal at the best meter reading

When the station has been identified, switch back to ADF and this brings in the loop which activates the radio compass pointer. If the tuning proves difficult, as with older sets, generally because the tuner is out of alignment, tune the frequency with ADF selected, so that you can get a rough indication when the pointer is homing on the station, then switch back to ANT for identification.

7. When satisfied that the station is correctly tuned, ensure ADF on, and press the test button. This rotates the loop and therefore deflects the pointer. On releasing the test button the pointer should return quickly to show the correct relative bearing of the beacon.

NOTES ON TUNING:

Never use an unidentified station, even though you are quite sure you have the right frequency.

Check that you do have the correct frequency and this is the station you want to use. It is possible to tune and use the wrong NDB.

Some ADF's are notoriously hard to tune, be patient and keep trying. The main difficulty seems to be that although the frequency is correct and the pointer appears to be pointing in the right direction, no ident is heard. Generally this is as a result of being too far away from the station for the ident signal to be strong enough and consequently the indications of the pointer are also unreliable.

Tuning errors can be caused by:-

1. Incorrect station selected
2. Aircraft too far away from NDB
3. Faulty or weak equipment
4. Interference from other stations
5. Signal distortion − night effect − coastal effect
6. Thunderstorm cells in proximity cause pointer to show where the storm is
7. Static, caused by aircraft passing through heavy rain
8. Check that you are not trying to use a locator or marker as an en route beacon from 100 miles away
9. Check from the map or chart that the pointer appears to point in approximately the known direction of the NDB.

Check and double check, keep the ident tuned in and do ensure that the morse identification is correct and not just any old morse. Check that the pointer can move and hasn't simply got stuck.

TO FIND THE QDM (MAGNETIC HEADING TO STEER TO THE STATION WITHOUT WIND:)

During the exercises no further mention of the RMI will be made. This is to avoid confusion, because the fixed compass rose is by far the commonest type still in use, and if you can fully understand the use of this type you should not have much difficulty in using the RMI.

When the pilot looks at his instrument, it is upright in the panel, and he must therefore learn to read it like this. However, in order to assist the student, there is, where necessary, a bonus compass rose orientated with the aircraft to assist you with the visual picture of what is going on. This visual orientation should, in fact, become a natural way for you to see the mental picture after a time.

FINDING THE QDM:

Tune and ident the NDB
Satisfy yourself that it is correctly tuned
Turn the function switch to ADF

The pointer will now indicate the direction of the beacon in relation to the nose of the aircraft. This indication, is, of course, the relative bearing.

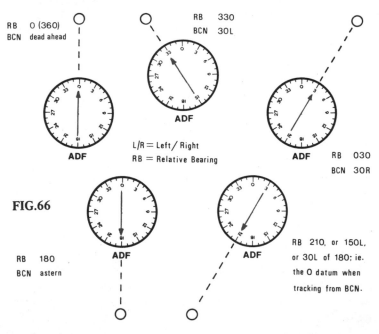

FIG.66

In all these situations the ADF is indicating the relative bearing, but the QDM will depend on the heading of the aircraft. From now on the ADF will be used in an unbreakable partnership with the Direction Indicator, and the best way to introduce this wedding of instruments is to look at the previous examples, this time showing heading and the position of the aircraft with relation to the beacon. You will see in each example that there are three ways of finding the QDM.

1. Add the relative bearing to the heading and the product of these equals the QDM, unless this number comes to more than 360, in which case subtract 360 to get the answer.

Heading 330°, Relative Bearing 330. ADD = 660 (blast)! this is more than 360 so 660 - 360 = 300. QDM = 300°.

2. Add or subtract the number of degrees the pointer has deviated left or right of centre, to or from the heading. Add if pointer right, subtract if pointer left.

Heading 330°, ADF pointer 330, or 30° left of 0, so subtract from heading, 330 = 300° QDM.

3. By transferring, in our imagination, the ADF pointer to the direction indicator. This is not an exact method, but is practical enough in certain circumstances.

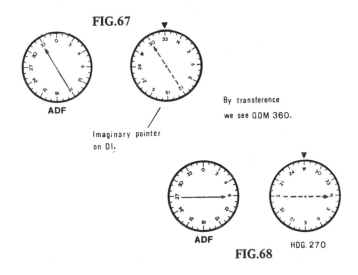

FIG.67

ADF

By transference
we see QDM 360.

Imaginary pointer
on DI.

ADF

FIG.68

HDG. 270

Use the method that seems best to you under the circumstances. Now let's look at those examples and in each case see the various possibilities for finding the QDM.

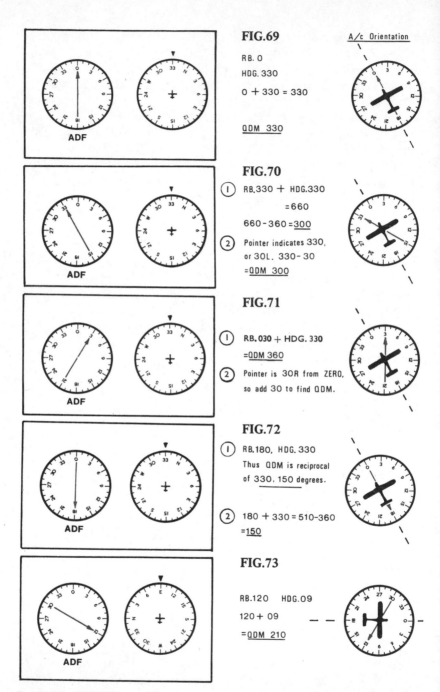

FIG.69

RB. 0

HDG. 330

0 + 330 = 330

QDM 330

A/c Orientation

FIG.70

(1) RB.330 + HDG.330

= 660

660 - 360 = 300

(2) Pointer indicates 330,

or 30L. 330 - 30

= QDM 300

FIG.71

(1) RB.030 + HDG. 330

= QDM 360

(2) Pointer is 30R from ZERO,

so add 30 to find QDM.

FIG.72

(1) RB.180, HDG. 330

Thus QDM is reciprocal

of 330, 150 degrees.

(2) 180 + 330 = 510 - 360

= 150

FIG.73

RB.120   HDG.09

120 + 09

= QDM 210

ADF

In each of these cases, it is not too difficult to imagine the ADF pointer on the DI, and get a quick visual on the QDM.

POSITION LINES

Having found the QDM, we wish to convert it into a position line.

1. Tune and identify
2. Obtain the QDM

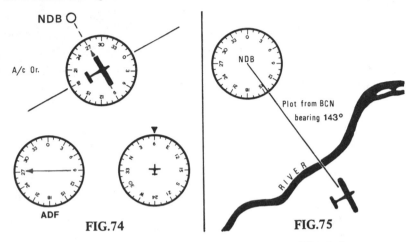

NDB

A/c Or.

ADF

FIG.74

Plot from BCN
bearing 143°

RIVER

FIG.75

Hdg. 060º ADF pointer is on Rel. Brg 270, or 90º left.

Hdg. 060º + Rel. Brg. 270º = 330º QDM.

3. The next step is to convert the magnetic bearing into a true bearing. Our heading of 060º is magnetic: if the variation is 7º west, our true heading is 053º. Now 053º represents the nose of the aircraft and the relative bearing of 270º is + 270 onto 053º. Answer 323º.

Thus the magnetic QDM minus the westerly variation equals the true bearing.

4. Plot or draw on your map the reciprocal of 323º, which is 143º.

5. 143º is the line to draw from the NDB and the aircraft is somewhere along this line, subject to the accuracy of the bearing. If you can combine this line with another bearing or visual feature, then you can, under ideal circumstances, call it a fix.

FLYING THE DIRECT TRACK FROM YOUR PRESENT POSITION TO OVERHEAD THE BEACON:
1. Tune and identify the beacon.
2. Ascertain the QDM.
3. Turn the aircraft onto the indicated QDM. This should

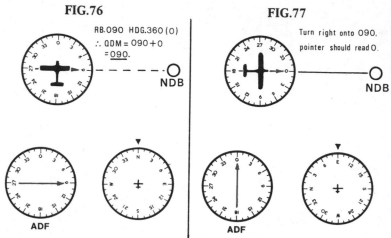

FIG.76

RB.090 HDG.360(0)
∴ QDM = 090 + 0
= 090.

NDB

ADF

FIG.77

Turn right onto 090,
pointer should read 0.

NDB

ADF

coincide with the Radio Compass Pointer on the '0' mark.
4. With the pointer on 0, the station is dead ahead.
5. We can now fly to the beacon by keeping the pointer on the 0 position. If the pointer deflects to the right, we simply turn right until it is again dead ahead. You may have observed, without any prompting from me, that this will result in a change of heading, and every time we turn to keep the pointer zeroed, we again alter the heading.

FIG.78

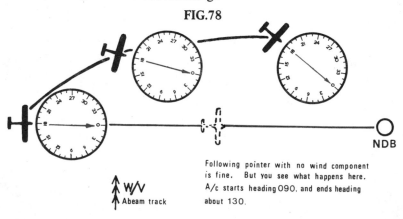

NDB

W/V
Abeam track

Following pointer with no wind component
is fine. But you see what happens here.
A/c starts heading 090, and ends heading
about 130.

PASSING THE BEACON:

As we reach a position of close proximity to the beacon, we shall find that the pointer tends to liven up. Having established yourself inbound to the beacon, do not make large and slavish over-corrections to the heading, close into the NDB. Obey the indications of the pointer, but by increments of 5º – 10º, not 20º – 30º. Passing the beacon is indicated by the pointer 'falling'. That is reversing from the '0' position and changing to 180º.

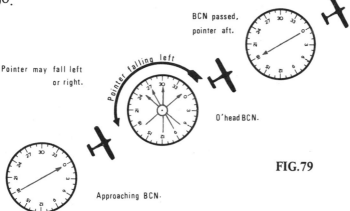

Pointer may fall left or right.

Pointer falling left

BCN passed, pointer aft.

O'head BCN.

Approaching BCN.

FIG.79

If the pointer falls rapidly, this indicates that the aircraft has passed directly over the station. A slower changing of the relative bearing shows that the aircraft is passing the beacon slightly abeam and which side is indicated by the pointer. A very slow rate of change in the relative bearing is a sign that we have definately missed the target, but this should not be by more than a mile when homing to an airways beacon, and much less when involved in a beacon approach. For the purpose of reporting over the beacon, use the 09 or 270 indication. This also holds good for starting the timing.

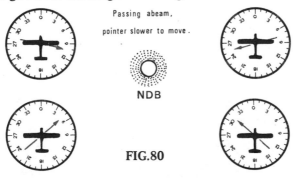

Passing abeam, pointer slower to move.

NDB

FIG.80

FLYING AWAY FROM THE STATION

When flying away from the beacon, we have a new datum position. The new datum is 180, and this is the point at which certain subtleties rear their grisly heads. The first one is the loss of the zero as the reference point. This problem is soon overcome by simply thinking of 180 as 0, and then translating deviations of the pointer into right or left of the 180 position.

Using the arrowhead of the pointer on 180, we can obey it, and if it shows a turn right — do it, and if it says turn left — do it, in the same way as you should obey the Ten Commandments.

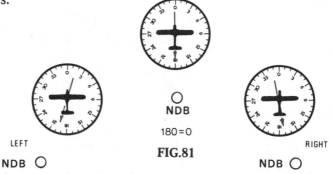

NDB

180=0

LEFT

RIGHT

FIG.81

NDB ◯   NDB ◯

Perhaps you have already observed the approach of the next problem. If we follow the pointer, turning left for instance, this places the needle even further to the left, and this difficulty leads us gently towards the higher realms of being able to use the ADF to intercept tracks and fly them with or without wind.

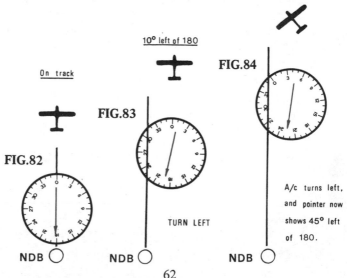

10° left of 180

FIG.84

On track

FIG.83

FIG.82

TURN LEFT

A/c turns left, and pointer now shows 45° left of 180.

NDB ◯   NDB ◯   NDB ◯

62

MAINTAINING THE REQUIRED TRACK AND COMPENSATING FOR DRIFT

In still air we can maintain our inbound track by keeping the pointer on 'O'. This will result in the a/c flying a fairly constant heading to the beacon, and will also hold true if we were heading directly into, or directly downwind.

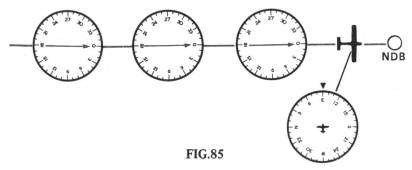

FIG.85

Calm conditions seldom exist at all levels, so we are obliged to develop our skills beyond this relatively simple stage, and take a big step forward. Unless the station is dead ahead and the aircraft is on track, we have to contend, not only with a DI whose heading differs from the track required, but also an ADF pointer which does not point at zero just because we are on track.

The ingredients of this navigational jelly, wobble gently together until we get them in exactly the right proportions, when they firm up into something more tangible. These ingredients are:

The track required

The aircraft heading

The position of the ADF pointer.

The track required is known, and it is a question of relating the difference between it and the other two.

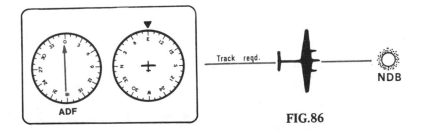

FIG.86

If the aircraft is on track, the pointer's deviation from '0' will be equal, but opposite to the amount that the Direction Indicator deviates from the required track.

If the heading and track are the same, and the pointer reads '0', then the aircraft is on track, as shown previously.

If the required track is 090, but the heading is 100, which is +10⁰, or ten degrees more than the track, then the pointer must read -10, or 350, for the aircraft to be on track. Plus 10 on DI means -10 on ADF. Any disagreement of this plus/minus relationship indicates that the aircraft is not on the required track.

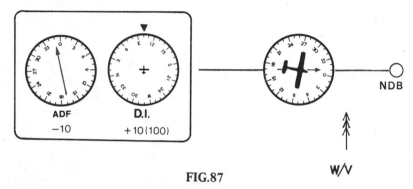

ADF   D.I.
−10   +10(100)

FIG.87

W/V

Taking a more extreme case. Required track 090⁰, Heading 360⁰. DI is therefore reading -90⁰, or 90 less than track, so we are looking for +90 on the ADF. This plus 90⁰ will indicate that we are on track, or crossing the track.

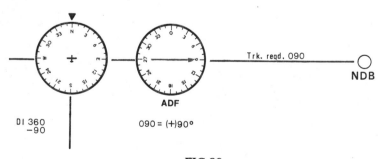

Trk. reqd. 090

NDB

ADF

DI 360
−90

090 = (+)90⁰

FIG.88

Can you see this clearly? When drift or angles of interception have to be allowed for, we know that we are on track when the deviation of the pointer is equal and opposite to the difference between the required track and the heading.

In the next example we shall be intercepting the track, and although this manoeuvre is enacted in greater detail later, it is necessary to introduce the subject here, if only to get back onto track after being blown off it by the wind.

Required track	030°
Present QDM	030°
W/V	300/20
Heading	030°

Beautiful things happen in three's, and the aircraft is on track.

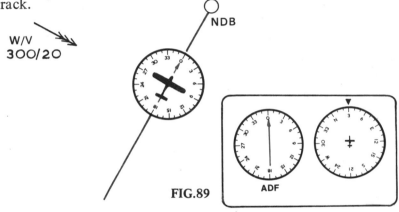

FIG.89

However, all is not well – the wind is about to drift us to the right (see Fig. 90). Heading is still 030° but ADF pointer indicates we are right of track, and is showing 10° left, or 350°. Problem: to regain track and maintain it. The best way to regain a track is to alter heading by at least double the indicated error. In this case 10°. Turn left 20°. Heading is now 010°, and as we altered the relative bearing of the NDB by 20°, the pointer shows a deviation of 20° from its present indication. As we turned left, the deviation of the pointer will be to the right; 010° on the bearing indicator. The situation is not too difficult to grasp. We are minus twenty on the DI, so we are looking for plus twenty on the ADF. As soon as we get plus twenty, we know we are back on track. To maintain the track it looks as though we should make our heading 020°. This is allowing 10° for drift. As the track is 030° and we are steering 020°, which is minus 10 on the DI, we are looking for plus 10, or 10 on the ADF, and this is now the datum point instead of zero. We now obey the pointer in relation to this new datum, turning left or right as indicated.

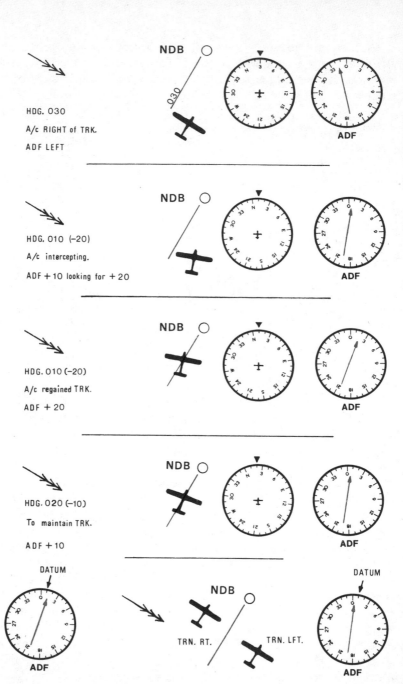

HDG. 030
A/c RIGHT of TRK.
ADF LEFT

NDB

ADF

HDG. 010 (–20)
A/c intercepting.
ADF + 10 looking for + 20

NDB

ADF

HDG. 010 (–20)
A/c regained TRK.
ADF + 20

NDB

ADF

HDG. 020 (–10)
To maintain TRK.
ADF + 10

NDB

ADF

DATUM

ADF

NDB

TRN. RT.

TRN. LFT.

DATUM

ADF

DATUM NOW 010 ON ADF

FIG.90

66

One of the main difficulties regarding the use of the ADF is recognising, quickly, which way to turn. Here is a final example which might help you deal with this problem.

Track required	150o
Aircraft heading	140o
ADF Pointer	0

Say to yourself, "I am heading 140o. This is 10o less than track required. As I am minus 10o on DI, I am looking for plus 10o on the Radio Compass. But ADF pointer reads 0. Think of 0 as being 10o left of +10, (which is the datum point in the course) and therefore turn left.

1. Decide difference between heading and track.
2. Decide where the datum should be.
3. See where the pointer is in relationship to this datum.
4. Turn the aircraft in direction indicated.

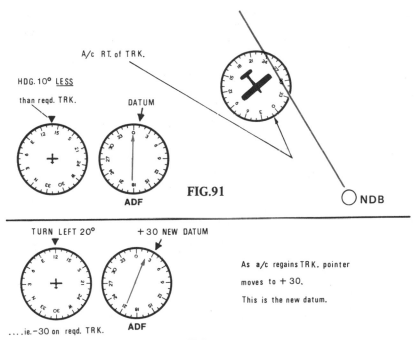

A/c RT. of TRK.

HDG. 10° LESS
than reqd. TRK.

DATUM

FIG.91

ADF

○ NDB

TURN LEFT 20°   +30 NEW DATUM

As a/c regains TRK. pointer
moves to + 30.
This is the new datum.

....ie. -30 on reqd. TRK.   ADF

FIG.92

Heading is now minus 30, so when pointer reaches the plus 30, we are back on track and should turn right 30o +/- the expected drift allowance to maintain it.

TRACKING FROM THE BEACON, AND ALLOWING FOR DRIFT

The difference between inbound and outbound tracking is simply that the pointer is in the opposite quadrant of the ADF instrument.

FIG.93

When tracking in, it is advisable to make a definate note of the picture you expect to see after you have passed the NDB.

As long as track and drift are the same after the beacon, as they were before, then you can expect the pointer's arrowhead to reverse and take up the present position of the arrows tail. Apart from this, having passed the beacon, divorce your mind from the 'to' situation, and think of 180 as zero, and then everything to the right is minus, and to the left plus.

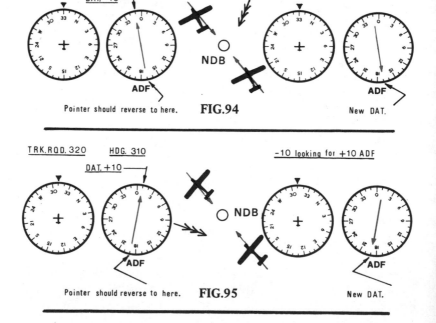

68

Regaining the track when the station is behind you is more difficult until you get used to it. Remember that when flying away from the station, with the pointer indicating a fly left signal, after we have turned left the pointer will show an even greater deviation than before. However, by applying the same rules as previously, we will eventually overcome our natural confusion at trying to do things the wrong way round.

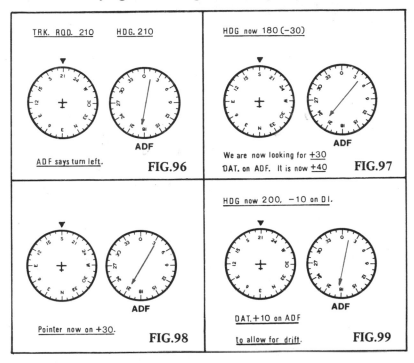

TRK. RQD. 210   HDG. 210

ADF

ADF says turn left.

FIG.96

HDG now 180 (−30)

ADF

We are now looking for +30
DAT. on ADF. It is now +40   **FIG.97**

ADF

Pointer now on +30.

FIG.98

HDG now 200, −10 on DI.

ADF

DAT. +10 on ADF

to allow for drift.   **FIG.99**

The track required is 210º (see above) and in fact the aircraft is heading 210º. The ADF pointer, however, is showing 10º left turn. The aircraft is now turned onto a heading of 180º. This is -30º. The pointer was reading 10º left but is now reading 40º left. This is made up from the original deviation of 10 + the 30 we have just turned. The new datum is now +30, and when the pointer reaches it, the aircraft is turned back onto course, but this time allowing 10º for possible or actual drift.

If we had found that the angle of interception had not brought us back onto the track, and the pointer had moved even further away from the datum; then this means we must take an even bigger bite and attack at an even greater angle.

INTERCEPTING A REQUIRED TRACK TO A BEACON

We will often be required to intercept an inbound or outbound track, to or from a beacon. This might be a standard departure, an Airways join, or a Letdown procedure, and all require some accurate and intelligent flying from the Captain. If you get the chance to watch your flying superiors playing these games, you will notice that even they are concentrating like mad to get it all exactly right.

Intercepting a track presents several variables which, mixed together, form a problem to be solved. Air speed, ground speed, wind velocity, distance from station. The first step to be decided is the angle of interception. This may be laid down in the procedure, or given to us as an instruction by Air Traffic.

We have already dealt with these problems in the VOR section, but briefly again, it depends on how quickly we want to achieve the track, our distance from the track and the beacon itself, and of course, the effect of wind. On nearing the track, we will decide by how many degrees we wish to anticipate the turn onto it. This anticipation of the turn is called lead. Lead is the quantity of degrees that we feel we should commence the turn in advance of the pointer reaching the on track datum. This lead is usually necessary in order to intercept the track as we complete the turn onto the final track heading. For example, 10° of lead means that we start turning 10° before the ADF pointer reaches the required + or - datum.

Making an exact join at 50 miles or more is not a matter to get excited about, but when manoeuvring nearer the beacon to execute a let down procedure, we need to have a mental picture of how distance, speed and wind, affect the amount of lead required. The closer you are to the station, the greater amount of lead required.

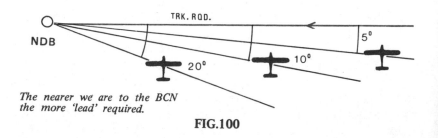

The nearer we are to the BCN
the more 'lead' required.

FIG.100

The direction of the wind in relation to the track we are about to intercept is another factor. In the previous illustration a northerly wind would cause the Captain to allow less lead than a southerly wind, which would be shoving him up to, and through the track. The amount of lead is also varied by the angle at which you decide to intercept the track. It is desirable that the final angle should be no greater than 45º.

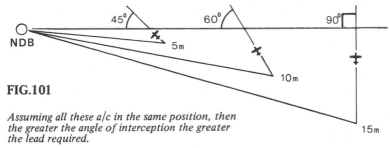

FIG.101

Assuming all these a/c in the same position, then the greater the angle of interception the greater the lead required.

We simply apply the lead we think we require to the datum and start the turn when the pointer reaches this position. We also get a good idea of the time to start the turn by watching the rate at which the pointer is moving over the dial.

Track required	265º
Wind velocity	300/20
Ground speed	120 knots

Point of interception from beacon about 5 nm.

If the aircraft is about seven miles south east of the track, we will turn right onto a heading of about 310º, thus making an angle of plus 45. The datum is now minus 45. If we decide that the lead is to be 5º, then the turn will commence when the pointer reaches the minus 40 position, or 5º ahead of the datum.

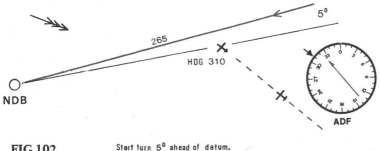

FIG.102   Start turn 5º ahead of datum.

INTERCEPTING TRACK FROM A STATION

This is basically the same as the previous exercise, with the principal difference that the pointer is now behind you.

Track required	090o
Heading	030o (-60o)

We are now looking for plus 60o on the ADF, which is 180 + 60 = 240o on ADF.

This time we want to allow 10o of lead, so we will start the turn at 250o, 10o before the pointer reaches 240o. Remember the pointer is falling from greater to less.

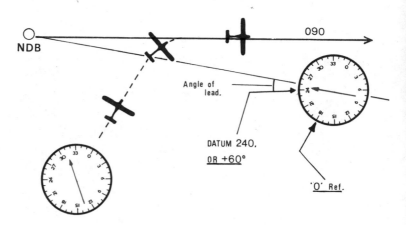

FIG.103

CHECKING POSITION AND G/S USING ADF

We have already seen the way this is done using the VOR, so it is only necessary to see how the same thing can be done using the ADF.

1. First we must obtain a bearing from a suitable ground station. The station we choose should be as near to a right angle from our track as possible.

2. The bearing we get will be a relative bearing, so we convert into a QDM, followed by a true bearing, and then plot the reciprocal of the true bearing from the station.

1. Hdg 142º M
   Relative bearing 060º
   QDM 202º − 7 (VAR. M)
   True bearing 195º
   Plot reciprocal of 195 = 015º

2. Hdg 142º M
   Relative bearing 120º
   QDM 262º − 7 (VAR. M)
   True bearing 255º
   Plot reciprocal of 255 = 075º

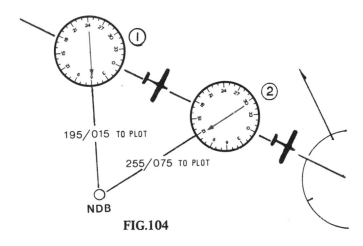

195/015 TO PLOT

255/075 TO PLOT

NDB

FIG.104

To find the G/S from these position lines, you must start the stopwatch at 1, stop the stopwatch at 2, note the time taken and measure the distance flown.

PROCEDURE AND HOLDING TURNS USING THE ADF

When making a turn onto an inbound track, whether it is on airways, in the hold, or during a procedure turn, we need to translate the pointers information quickly and correctly.

We will be looking to see if, when we complete the turn, we will be on track, overshooting it or undershooting it. In fact we gather this information from the pointer and direction indicator before the turn is completed, so that action can be taken to remedy any tendency to miss the track by a significant amount.

The basis of this exercise is the "60/30" check. We mean by this, that we check the progress of the ADF pointer against the direction indicator at sixty degrees, and at thirty degrees, before reaching the inbound heading. The ADF pointer should show, within a very few degrees, the same number of degrees still to go as are indicated on the DI.

For example, suppose we are turning from an outbound leg of 090° inbound to the beacon on the required QDM of 270°. The first question is, are we turning left onto track or are we turning right. When turning right onto track, the 60/30 headings are always less than the required QDM. So in this case they will be 210/240. When the aircraft heading passes 210° on the DI, the ADF pointer should read + 60, and when the aircraft passes the 240° on the DI, the pointer should be passing the +30. When turning left onto the QDM, then the 60/30 check points are at greater values than the QDM.

FIG.105   **FIG.106**

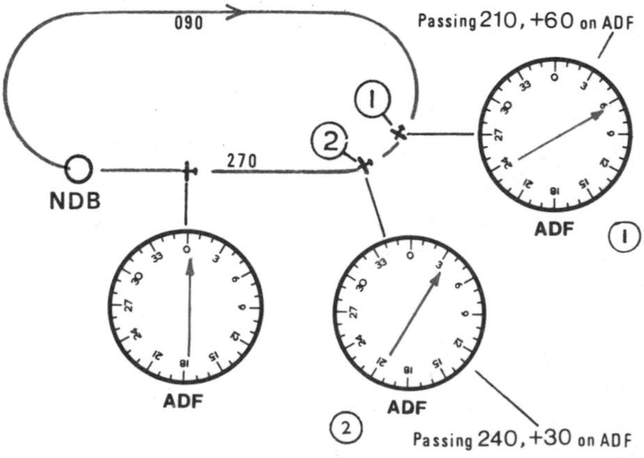

74

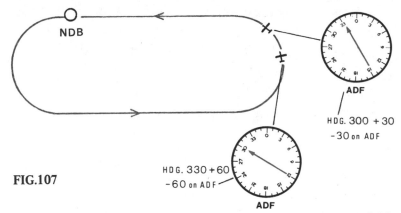

FIG.107

HDG. 300 + 30
−30 on ADF

ADF

HDG. 330 + 60
−60 on ADF

ADF

In this case 330º would be the 60º check point, and 300º the 30º check point. Also please note that the 60/30 check is given by the ADF pointer when it is on '300' and '330' on the compass rose.

UNDERSHOOTING

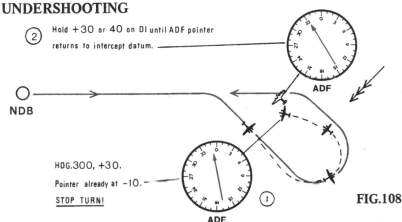

② Hold +30 or 40 on DI until ADF pointer returns to intercept datum.

ADF

NDB

HDG.300, +30.
Pointer already at −10.
STOP TURN!

ADF

① **FIG.108**

Here we are, turning left onto 270º QDM during a procedure turn. The wind, as you can see, is from the north east, although this is only one of several reasons that might cause us to undershoot. The undershoot is indicated by the ADF pointer coming up to the zero in advance of the heading being achieved on the DI. Thus at the 60º check the ADF pointer may have only 40º to go. And at the 30º check, only 10º to go.

The correction for an undershoot is to stop the turn at around the 30º check point, and to maintain a steady heading to make the interception of your required QDM as quickly as possible.

If in this case we stop the turn at +30 on the DI, when the ADF pointer reads -10, we are waiting for the pointer to return to the -30 position to tell us that we are now back on track.

NOTE: Not only must you stop the turn, but it may be necessary to turn back 10, 20 or even more degrees to rectify the error and regain the track.

OVERSHOOTING THE TRACK

In the same let down or hold situation, with a wind behind us, we are very likely to overshoot the track. This is indicated on the ADF by the pointer failing to reach the zero position and lagging behind the 60/30 check. The pointer will probably be in the right place at the 60 check, but instead of progressing steadily forward to the 30/0 point, it starts to go backwards to the 30 or 60 mark again. All we can do in this case is to continue the turn past the inbound QDM and back towards the track to intercept it in the usual way. Remember that undershooting or overshooting, or even rolling out on the correct QDM we should have already decided the heading we require to maintain the inbound track. Keeping the w/v in mind, roll out of the turn directly onto the heading that you think is most likely to keep you on the track.

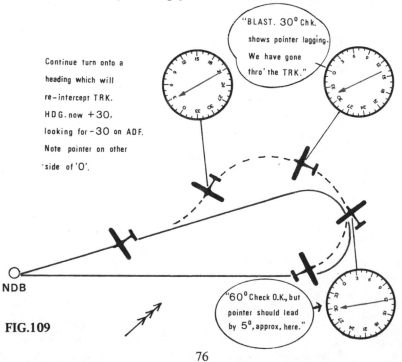

FIG.109

HOLDING PATTERNS WITH ADF

Again, we have dealt with the basics with the VOR, so all we need to do here is to see what sort of indications we expect to get from the ADF.

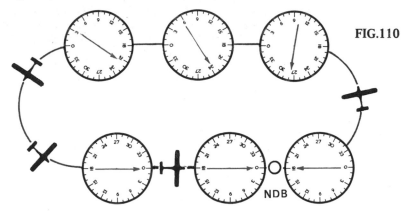

FIG.110

With no wind to fight, the hold will look something like this.

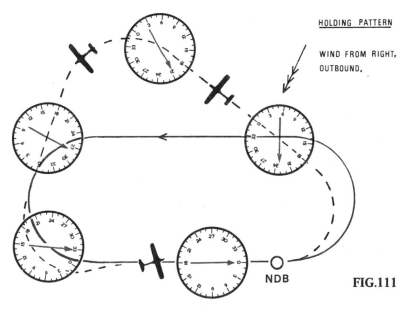

HOLDING PATTERN

WIND FROM RIGHT,
OUTBOUND.

NDB

FIG.111

Wind causes most of the problems in the hold. Try to assess the drift on the first inbound to the beacon and then treble it into wind on the outbound leg. The positions of the pointer do not help a great deal until turning back onto the inbound again.

Then we use the 60/30 check on the turn and take appropriate action if we feel we are undershooting, or overshooting the inbound track. In the above Fig. 109 we overshot and kept the turn going to re-intercept the track. An undershoot would mean stopping the turn and even increasing our angle of interception. Remember, we are working very close to the beacon in holds and let downs and so if you are sure you have missed the track, you must try to re-establish yourself on it before reaching the beacon and the next manoeuvre. So, as circumstances demand, strong winds, or misjudged turns; attack the track positively, very easily said, not so easily done.

EQUIPMENT FAULTS

1. Static and electrical activity deflect the needle towards active thunderstorms.
2. Precipitation static caused by aircraft flying through areas of heavy rain, reduces reliability of signal.
3. Interference from other stations, or sky waves, mainly evening to early morning and most severe dawn and dusk, because this is when ionic changes are at their greatest.
4. Bearings taken across a coastline from an aircraft out to sea, using an inland station. The radio wave bends as it crosses the coast due to the difference in the conductivity between earth and water. Under these circumstances the aircraft's equipment will give a misleading readout.

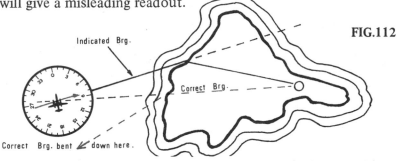

Indicated Brg.

Correct Brg.

Correct Brg. bent down here.

FIG.112

5. No warning flags to give the Captain instant fault recognition. Keep checking ident, deflection knob and pointer response. Don't go all gaga looking at your superbly centralised pointer, it may have got stuck or just switched off.
6. You must be within the published range.

PILOT FAULTS:

1. Wrong station tuned, wrong frequency selected.
2. Failure to identify and verify the station.
3. Failure to carry out pre-flight checks, and airborne checks.
4. Flying the pointer to the station rather than flying the track.
5. Not using the DI in constant conjunction with the ADF.
6. Over correction when very close to the station.
7. Failure to mentally establish the drift angle.
8. Trying to fly accurately with an unsynchronised Direction Indicator.
9. No NDB station should be used, and/or relied upon unless identified, checked, and cross checked with other instruments or by reference to a map.
10. When meteorological conditions are unfavourable, when pointer hunts and won't settle down.

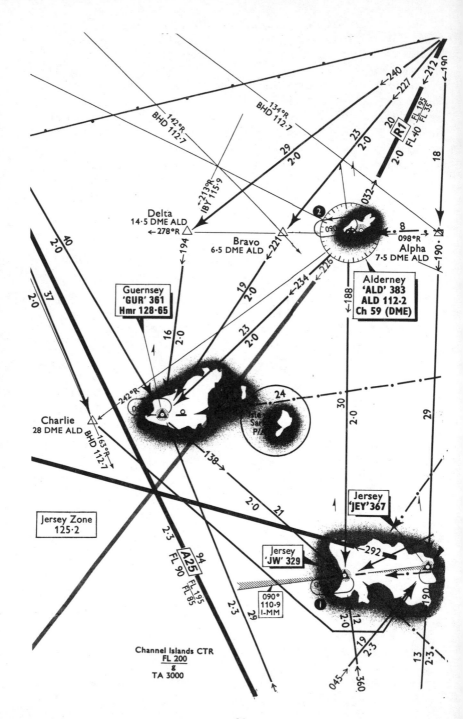

ADF APPROACH AT JERSEY

(In the circumstances given below Jersey would probably not accept special VFR traffic).

Aircraft G-CASE

Overhead Alderney at 3000 feet, inbound from Shoreham

Wind velocity at this altitude 300/20

Wind velocity at Jersey 280/12

Weather at Jersey, 4kms in drizzle, 2 @ 400', 4 @ 600', 8 @ 800'.

Thinks – "Why am I coming to Jersey?"

The aircraft is cleared down to 2000', and is to call when overhead the JEY beacon and commencing the outbound leg of the procedure. No hold is anticipated, but it is advisable to have an idea of what to do if there is.

Write down the QNH and QFE. Set altimeters as required.

Extract the Chart.

Note that from our present position we can make a direct entry into the hold, or let down procedure. We go straight into the procedure from overhead the beacon, and we are already half way round the first turn. So after passing the beacon we will continue on the present heading for about 25 seconds before starting the turn.

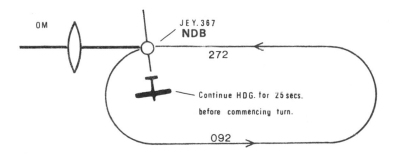

FIG.113

Wind velocity 300/20. Allow quarter drift on each track, but this must be multiplied on the outbound track of 092. Three times for the hold, twice for the direct procedure should be sufficient.

¼ drift is ¼ of total windspeed, which is 5 for a wind velocity of 20 kts and an airspeed of 100 - 120 kts.

81

Timing on the outbound leg of the hold would be about 45 seconds, or 1 min 10 secs from the beacon (25+45). If no hold is required we see from the timing box at the bottom of the chart that we must fly outbound for one minute in still air.

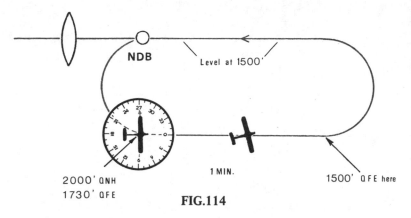

2000' QNH
1730' QFE

1 MIN.

1500' QFE here

FIG.114

Complete all checks before you reach the beacon as there's one hell of a lot to do afterwards.

Note that the OCL is 500', so we arrive at an MDA of 700'.

Note the overshoot procedure. Climb straight ahead to 1900'.

Note timing on final from outer marker to threshold. If we assume that the average wind speed on the approach is 16 kts and our TAS will be 100 kts, then groundspeed will be about 85 kts. Go to the timing tables at the bottom of the chart and interpolate roughly between the 90 box and the 70 box. The difference is 69 seconds, add a third of this to the 90 box and we can allow 4 mins 23 seconds from NDB JEY to threshold.

Runway magnetic heading is 272°, so we can anticipate about 10 degrees of drift from the right.

Note also that when we make the inbound turn on to the runway QDM, we shall be turning left 'so that the 60/30 check will be at 272 + 60° and 272° + 30°. This will therefore be at 332° and 302°.

Absorb as much pre-flight information on a let down as you possibly can, and polish off the fine points in your mind before arrival over the beacon.

All checks completed prior to arrival at the beacon.

Overhead the beacon:

start the stopwatch and

call Air Traffic that you are overhead give your height and hold heading 180°for 25 seconds
commence descent to 1505 feet QFE.

At the end of 25 seconds, turn left onto 080º, and continue at 1500'. At 1 minute 25 seconds from the beacon, or 1 minute from commencing the outbound leg, turn left again.

During the turn, maintain height and check the DI against the pointer at 332 and 302. If you are undershooting, stop the turn. If overshooting, continue the turn and return to the inbound QDM.

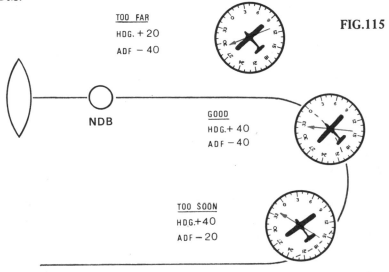

TOO FAR
HDG. + 20
ADF − 40

NDB

GOOD
HDG.+ 40
ADF − 40

TOO SOON
HDG.+40
ADF − 20

FIG.115

The turn onto final should be stopped on a heading of about 280º to allow for drift. If you are on track after the turn, the ADF pointer will settle on -10 as the heading is +10 to the track.

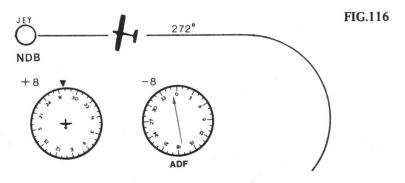

JEY
NDB

272°

+8

−8

ADF

FIG.116

Maintain the correct QDM to the beacon and note the position of the pointers tail. This is where the pointers arrowhead should reverse to, after passing the beacon.

Overhead the JEY beacon on the inbound leg, recommence the descent at about 400' per minute, and restart the stopwatch. Do not go below the height of 1290' QFE, before reaching the outer marker. Obey the indications of the pointer if it moves left or right of the 170 datum.

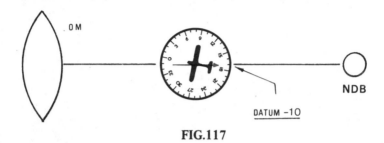

FIG.117

Once past the outer marker you are clear to continue down to the MDA of 600 feet. Wind direction is backing as we go through the last 1200 feet or so. Be ready for this and don't hesitate to change heading if the ADF indicates that you should. On this approach, it is likely that the wind is going to give less drift as we lose height.

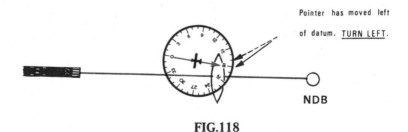

FIG.118

On reaching 600 feet, level off, maintain QDM and check the stopwatch for time to field. If the clock says 3 minutes 50 seconds, then we have about 22 seconds to find the runway. Look ahead and slightly to each side, it may not be dead ahead. If on looking outside and away from your instruments all is IMC, do not be tempted to nudge it down a few more feet, this not only defeats the object of weather minima, but once you violate this boundary of safety, you are all set for a classic case of crashitus. If you ensure that you do not go below MDA, you also ensure that you don't fly when the weather is likely to be well below your limits. If you can see the ground, but no runway, at the end of the time, overshoot. You must plan your flights so that you carry enough fuel to hold, for say 30 minutes, have another go, and go to an alternate. There should also be 100% certainty that conditions will enable you to get into one of your chosen airfields.

APPENDIX ONE: APPROACH DESCENT.

Minimum Descent Altitude (MDA), is the lowest height to which the aircraft may descend, unless the crew are able to see at least some segment of the approach lights or runway. It is essential to ensure that you identify the lights as runway lights, before landing in the Birmingham Bull Ring.

VOR/NDB approaches are not considered to be precision approaches because they contain only intermittent vertical, or glide path information. For this reason, the minimum altitude is seldom less than 500 feet. There is nothing clever about getting into an airfield in conditions which you, the airfield, or the aircraft is not equipped to deal with. As a private operator you must lay your own guide lines, as nobody else will.

1. Never begin a flight if you have reason to believe that conditions will be outside the scope of your previous training and qualifications. It is not good enough to have had a couple of goes yourself.

2. Airfields without published let down patterns should be used only when there is good VMC. A VMC airfield is a VMC airfield, and regardless of the number of DME's and VOR's surrounding it, if it lacks official let down recognition, don't you try it, and don't let anybody else persuade you.

3. Calculate your own MDA for each approach on the basis of adding 200 feet to the OCL published on the chart. It is not advisable to attempt an approach if the visibility is less than 1500 metres, and this could be greater depending on the circumstances.

4. The descent must be carefully timed from some specific position so that the pilot knows that, when the calculated time is up, he must commence the overshoot unless the runway has been sighted

5. This timing is usually started from the beacon which is situated approximately four miles from the threshold on final approach. In some cases this is not the situation and it is located on the field itself. In these circumstances, you either have to start the timing on commencement of the outbound leg or continue at MDA until overhead the beacon on the field.

6. The rate of descent depends on the ground speed and can be arrived at by multiplying the first two digits of the estimated ground speed by 5.

Thus 090 kts = 5 x 9   = 45 or 450 feet per minute.
120 kts = 5 x 12 = 60 or 600 feet per minute
060 kts   5 x 6 = 30 or   300 feet per minute
070 kts   5 x 7 = 35 or   350 feet per minute
100 kts   5 x 10 = 50 or 500 feet per minute
150 kts   5 x 15 = 75 or 750 feet per minute

It is for you to decide the power setting that achieves this rate. However, it is not necessary to achieve the exact rate of descent. What is important is to get the aircraft down to MDA about 30 seconds before you estimate that you will be over the threshold.

Then fly the plane level until either the time is up and over shoot as necessary or the runway comes into sight.

APPENDIX TWO. DRIFT AND TIMING

There are several ways of finding solutions to the constant requirements of knowing drift, head and tailwind components. What you must be able to do, is to have some method of making a reasonably accurate first assessment, so that only small, final corrections are necessary.

Wind components are subject to many different factors with infinite variables. Wind speed and direction, aircraft heading, aircraft speed, track required. There are two things we can do. We can use a method to find the wind component and then work out how this will affect our particular aircraft in drift, or we can put an average airspeed for our aircraft on the slide rule computer, and obtain some figures of a general nature that will give us instant allowances for drift. Both systems must be treated as rough guides rather than exact solutions and the second method is only applicable to a narrow band of airspeeds. Finding the cross and head/tail wind component is probably the best, but having done it, we still need to know what proportion of the component equals the drift.

Wind component:

Angle of wind to track	Cross wind comp.	Head/tail wind comp.
0 - 30⁰	.5	.9
31 - 60⁰	.7	.7
61 - 90⁰	.9	.5

The first column shows the three basic angles. The second, cross wind component and the third, head or tail wind component.

Thus, if wind angle to track is 35⁰, and the wind velocity is 25 kts, we find that both cross wind and head/tail wind components are calculated at .7 of the wind speed. This equals 17.5. Head/tail component is decided according to whether the angle is fore or aft. This component is accurate at 30, 60 or 90 but between these angles, allowances must be made. The amount of drift involved will depend entirely on the airspeed and this is where some pre-knowledge of your own speeds, and how wind affects you at these speeds, is useful.

For aircraft carrying out procedures at between 100 and 120 kts, the amount of drift is about half of the wind component. 17.5 rounded up to 18, take half of this, giving drift of 9⁰.

Head or tail winds are compensated by knowing your G/S from the data given, or increasing/decreasing the time you hold a track, by the same number of seconds as the relevant component.

The other method is to take a narrow speed range for your aircraft and apply various wind situations to it on the CRP slide rule/computer. Again, we can take 100 - 120 kts, and produce a small table which gives us an instant read out of drift, head/tail wind component. The fractions are the proportions of the W/V to allow for drift and timing.

Angle	Drift	Head/Tail
0 - 30	1/4	All
31 - 60	1/3	1/2
61 - 90	1/2	0

Thus at W/V 295/20, and track required 260, we have an angle 35°. This gives drift as one third of wind speed and G/S reduced by half of the wind speed. All these indications are approximate, but practical. We therefore allow 7° of drift or three times this in the outbound leg of the hold, and subtract 10 kts from the G/S, in practical terms this means adding at least 10 seconds to the wind ward track.

QDM Magnetic Track to Station or Magnetic Heading to Steer
QDR Magnetic bearing from the station

The DME

DISTANCE MEASURING EQUIPMENT OR DME

The best way to read this section is in conjunction with a ½ million map showing VOR station points.

D.M.E. stands for Distance Measuring Equipment, and does exactly what it claims. It measures the distance from your aircraft to the appropriate DME facility. In most cases the DME is combined, or 'co-located' with VOR and the tuning frequency will be the same. Thus by selecting the VOR frequency the DME is also tuned. DAVENTRY VOR is tuned on 116.4 Mc/s and likewise is its associated DME. However on most types of equipment the DME is switched on and tuned using a separate box.

DME is generally used by the pilot in conjunction with a VOR in order to obtain a bearing or track, plus distance and this gives him a 'FIX' or an exact position.

A DME facility is indicated on the topographical map with a small symbol and a channel number. The two symbols shown in Fig. 1 are for a DME sitting all alone and unwedded to a VOR.

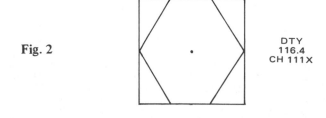

Fig. 1

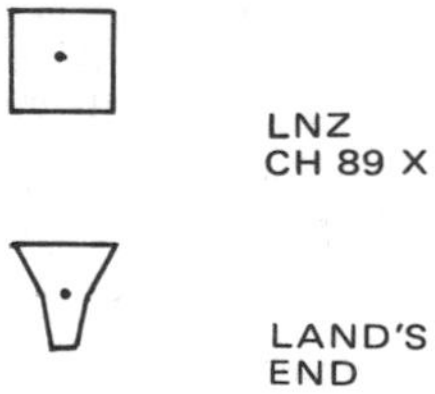

LNZ
CH 89 X

LAND'S
END

In a small box beside the symbol is shown the call sign 'LNZ', channel number, and most important the frequency. Note that there is a VOR at Lands End, but the DME is not located at the same spot. Fig. 2 shows the symbol for DAVENTRY VOR/DME, which like most DME's is co-located on the same spot as its VOR.

Fig. 2

DTY
116.4
CH 111X

DME's are most easily recognised by finding the channel numbers and the letters DME, under the VOR frequency. 111X at Daventry for example. These numbers refer to the internal workings of the equipment and need concern the pilot only in so far as he can tell that this is the position of a DME.

As already noted at Lands End, there are a certain number of stations which are not on the same position as the VOR with which they are associated. WALLASEY near Liverpool is another one of them. In these cases, although the frequency is the same as the VOR, the identification code has the last letter changed to a Z. This reminds the pilot that there are up to 5 miles difference between the VOR position and the DME. In any case the situation is made clear by looking carefully at the map before or during use. The best use of DME is made with the aid of Radio Navigation Charts as these give all the important ATC reporting points including bearing and distance.

THE EQUIPMENT:

In very simple terms the aircraft equipment asks the relevant DME ground station how far away it is? and the ground station sends back the correct answer.

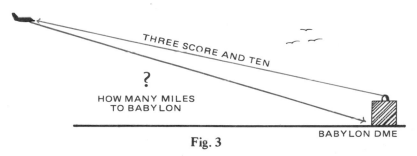

Fig. 3

The airborne equipment is housed in the usual small box of transistorised weirdness and is connected to an aerial situated on the belly of the aircraft. It may be that selecting the VOR will bring the DME set into operation, but you are more likely to have a completely different box to tune. In any case, to tune we.

(a) Switch ON.
(b) Select correct frequency.
(c) Check the identity of the station.
(d) Await a reading.

The important information of NM to go to the station or miles passed the station, will be shown to the pilot either on a dial or as numbers in a window, or yet again in pretty digital lights.

Having switched on and tuned the DME the equipment itself will operate in the Ultra High Frequency range or at about 1000 Mc/s. This is of no practical consequence to the pilot who only wishes to see the results. The airborne DME sends out a series of interrogatory pulses, which on reaching the ground station will trigger a reply pulse, which is transmitted in such a way that the aircraft equipment is able to recognise the reply to its own signal, and reject the replies meant for another aircraft.

Sounds fantastic, but think of a House Martin travelling 3000 miles one way and then 3000 miles back again to exactly the same corner of the same roof it last visited nine months ago. Distance is computed by measuring the time taken by the question and answer signal to return to the aircraft. This time, is translated into distance.

All this excitement under the bonnet is presented to the pilot in any one of a number of ways. As is usual with a good Navaid, if the equipment is out of range or giving trouble of one sort or another there should be some kind of indication that this is so. This might take the form of an 'OFF' flag, or a bar (red) which comes down in front of the numbers. The latest equipment simply does not show a reading at all if the equipment is not functioning.

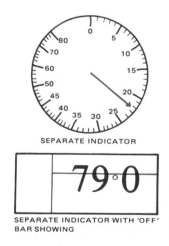

SEPARATE INDICATOR

SEPARATE INDICATOR WITH 'OFF' BAR SHOWING

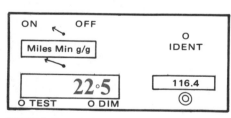

INTERGRATED DME SET
SHOWING NM AND TENTHS OF NM
ALSO MIN TO STATION OR GROUND SPEED

Fig. 4

NOTES ON CHARACTERISTICS AND OPERATION

1. DME likes to keep cool so do not leave it on unnecessarily whilst stationary.

2. They are short range, line of site instruments which follow roughly the same rules as VOR, but in fact they must be regarded as reduced in range capabilities. Their maximum range is about 200 NM but this depends on height. Whereas a VOR at 2000 feet may be useable under ideal circumstances from a distance of 60/70 NM, DME at this height is happier at 40/50 NM.

3. Some DME's tend to hunt for the correct distance. This is indicated by a continuous succession of numerals dancing before your eyes, or a ridiculous number which gradually changes into something more sensible. Many of the latest sets will lock on immediately, providing the range and height are within limits, but they may also suddenly lose the range and 'flip their lids' as it were. This might happen in a turn, at the limits of the range, or for no apparent reason.

4. Beware of the digital light indicator—although superb when working, they can throw a few wires and turn "0" into 8, 5 into a thunderstorm "$\digamma$" or 1 into 7 and 9 into "$\sqsubset$". This obviously means that some of their little wires have got mixed up and repairs are needed.

5. Already in this book we have advised against putting all your trust in these infernal machines. Use your own common sense all the time. So go through all the checks, monitor the readings. Ensure that they are sensible and agree roughly with your own deductions, that is if you have any idea of where you are at all. Having said this— Hooray for VOR with DME.!!

6. DME measures the slant distance between the ground station and the aircraft, so unless you decide to clobber the ground station, you are seldom going to get a zero reading in the cruise. If the DME is standing by an airport runway at which you are landing or taking off then the zero will appear when you are passing on the ground. The error between air, or DME distance, and ground distance is maximum over the station and minimum the further you are away from it. Error increases to maximum overhead, where it indicates your height.

93

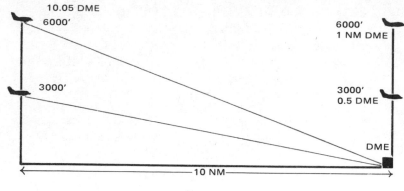

Fig. 5

Station passage will be shown by DME steadily reducing to show your eventual height overhead; at 3000 feet this would equal 0.5, at 2000 feet 0.3. Having done this it will then start increasing again. Obviously the VOR pointer and flags give the usual signs of having passed the station.

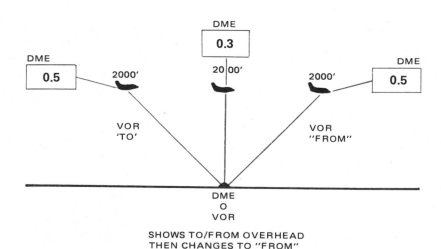

SHOWS TO/FROM OVERHEAD
THEN CHANGES TO "FROM"
AFTER PASSING STATION

Fig. 6

PRACTICAL USE OF DME

1. Distance to a VOR/DME. This is a simple exercise and needs little explanation. The DME will of course not only indicate the distance now, but also give a continuous picture of the decreasing or increasing miles.
2. When used in conjunction with VOR bearing information it gives a "fix" and a 'running fix'.

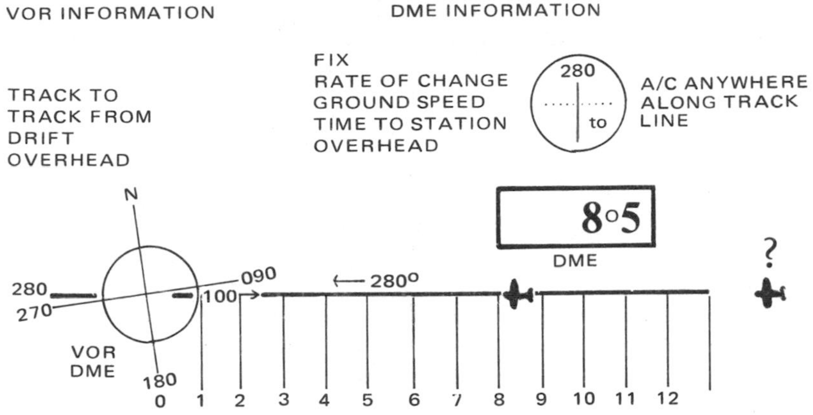

VOR INFORMATION   DME INFORMATION

```
                         FIX                  /  280  \     A/C ANYWHERE
TRACK TO                 RATE OF CHANGE       ( ....|.... )  ALONG TRACK
TRACK FROM               GROUND SPEED          \    |    /   LINE
DRIFT                    TIME TO STATION          to
OVERHEAD                 OVERHEAD
```

Fig. 7

Magnifico! It makes you feel really good to know exactly where you are. It is as if light has suddenly flooded a darkened room in which you know where the door is, but not how far you are from it. Instead of moving carefully forward, you can now step out boldly.

3. 'To' or 'from' distance can be read depending on which way you are going. Distance decreasing—To: Distance increasing—going from. Obvious I know, but there it is.
4. Providing you are moving directly towards or directly away from a DME, you can time the changing miles and calculate your ground speed. This can be done either by simple maths or if you have a tachymeter on your watch, just time one NM and read off the ground speed. The best sets do all this for you at the flick of a switch, and then add insult to injury by telling you how many minutes to reach the station at the present ground speed. Nothing much left for the pilot to think about except to keep ahead of his aircraft, and that is as it should be.

5. Position reports can now be made over the sea, highlands or moors, without having to take cross cuts or look down at unspecified objects known only to local boys. ORTAC, in the middle of nowhere—but 222° to GUR and 41 NM DME GUR—simple and blissful.

6. DME with VOR can also be used to find a position which is not itself served directly by either. This method is only for cruising flight and not for descents through low cloud.

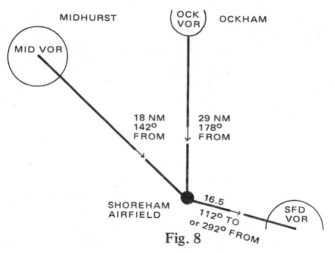

Fig. 8

7. DME can be used to avoid an obstacle or high ground.

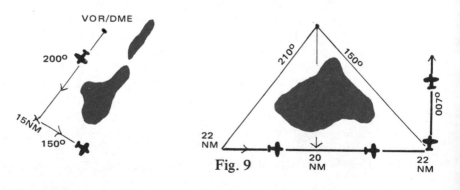

Fig. 9

8. The latest use to which DME is being harnessed is to couple it up with the VOR or ILS on an airfield. As yet this is only to be found at a few Airports. Guernsey is one of these twice blessed fields. Here is an opportunity to get "0.1" or even a zero reading on the indicator, as the DME is about half way down the runway on the north side of it. This DME can now be used as a major part of a let down procedure and particularly on the approach without the glideslope indicator. For example, with a DME reading of 2 NM, we should be at about 640 feet and 1 NM 320 feet. Outbound legs and holds can all be facilitated by using an airfield DME. At least we should not go screaming 20 NM downwind in the hold without noticing it on the DME. It is also surprising how much information regarding wind effect can be gained by watching the rate of change on the DME counter. As you go downwind outbound, you see the rapidly changing 10ths of a mile and you get used to the rhythm of change. As you commence your turn back into the wind it is very obvious by just watching the slower rate of change that you have turned into wind and the effect this is having on your aircraft speed over the ground.

TO SUMMARISE
1. Tunc and identify the station
2. Ensure correct station
3. Check any flag indications
4. Check type for DME/VOR—co-located or not co-located
5. Check initial readings are sensible
6. Use as appropriate
7. Before making a flight, measure and write down any useful DME distances, and make notes on the flight log or plan.
8. Remember it may go wrong at either ground or aircraft so try not to forget how to fly without it.
9. By going back to the VOR section of the book and putting a DME at all the VOR stations you can very soon get a useful idea of the various ways a DME can be utilised.

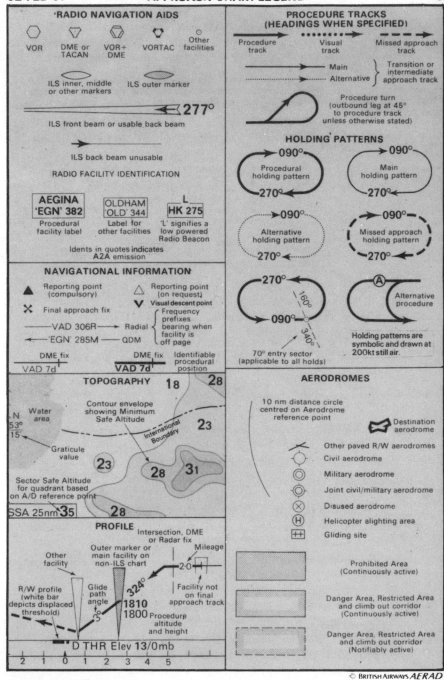

RADIO NAVIGATION AIDS

VOR　　DME or TACAN　　VOR+ DME　　VORTAC　　Other facilities

ILS inner, middle or other markers　　ILS outer marker

⟞⟞277°

ILS front beam or usable back beam

ILS back beam unusable

RADIO FACILITY IDENTIFICATION

AEGINA 'EGN' 382 — Procedural facility label

OLDHAM 'OLD' 344 — Label for other facilities

L HK 275 — 'L' signifies a low powered Radio Beacon

Idents in quotes indicates A2A emission

NAVIGATIONAL INFORMATION

▲ Reporting point (compulsory)

△ Reporting point (on request)

✕ Final approach fix

V Visual descent point

—— VAD 306R ——► Radial

◄—— 'EGN' 285M —— QDM

Frequency prefixes bearing when facility is off page

DME fix VAD 7d

DME fix VAD 7d — Identifiable procedural position

TOPOGRAPHY

18　28

N 53° 15' — Water area

Contour envelope showing Minimum Safe Altitude

International Boundary

23

Graticule value

23

28　31

Sector Safe Altitude for quadrant based on A/D reference point

SSA 25nm 35　28

PROFILE

Other facility

Outer marker or main facility on non-ILS chart

Intersection, DME or Radar fix

Mileage

2·0

R/W profile (white bar depicts displaced threshold)

Glide path angle

324°

1810
1800 Procedure altitude and height

Facility not on final approach track

D THR Elev 13/0mb

2　1　0　1　2　3　4　5

PROCEDURE TRACKS (HEADINGS WHEN SPECIFIED)

Procedure track　　Visual track　　Missed approach track

——► Main
·······► Alternative

Transition or intermediate approach track

Procedure turn (outbound leg at 45° to procedure track unless otherwise stated)

HOLDING PATTERNS

090° / 270° Procedural holding pattern

090° / 270° Main holding pattern

090° / 270° Alternative holding pattern

090° / 270° Missed approach holding pattern

270° / 090° — 160° / 340°

70° entry sector (applicable to all holds)

Ⓐ Alternative procedure

Holding patterns are symbolic and drawn at 200kt still air.

AERODROMES

10 nm distance circle centred on Aerodrome reference point

Destination aerodrome

╳ Other paved R/W aerodromes

⊕ Civil aerodrome

◉ Military aerodrome

◎ Joint civil/military aerodrome

⊗ Disused aerodrome

Ⓗ Helicopter alighting area

⊞ Gliding site

Prohibited Area (Continuously active)

Danger Area, Restricted Area and climb out corridor (Continuously active)

Danger Area, Restricted Area and climb out corridor (Notifiably active)

© BRITISH AIRWAYS *AERAD*

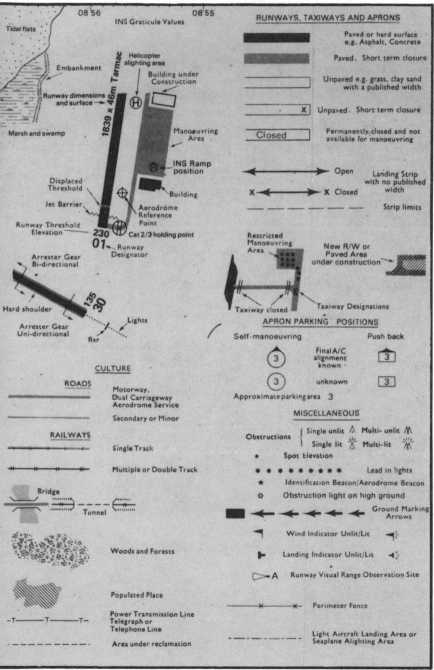

INS Graticule Values

08 56   08 55

Tidal flats

Embankment

Runway dimensions and surface

Marsh and swamp

Helicopter alighting area

Building under Construction

1839 x 46m Tarmac

Manoeuvring Area

INS Ramp position

Displaced Threshold

Building

Jet Barrier

Aerodrome Reference Point

Runway Threshold Elevation

230

Cat 2/3 holding point

01

Runway Designator

Arrester Gear Bi-directional

135

30

Hard shoulder

Lights

Arrester Gear Uni-directional

Bar

CULTURE

ROADS

Motorway, Dual Carriageway

Aerodrome Service

Secondary or Minor

RAILWAYS

Single Track

Multiple or Double Track

Bridge

Tunnel

Woods and Forests

Populated Place

Power Transmission Line
Telegraph or Telephone Line

-T——T——T-

Area under reclamation

RUNWAYS, TAXIWAYS AND APRONS

Paved or hard surface e.g. Asphalt, Concrete

Paved. Short term closure

Unpaved e.g. grass, clay sand with a published width

X   Unpaved. Short term closure

Closed   Permanently closed and not available for manoeuvring

Open   Landing Strip with no published width
X ◄———► X   Closed

——— ——— ———   Strip limits

Restricted Manoeuvring Area

New R/W or Paved Area under construction

Taxiway closed   Taxiway Designations

APRON PARKING POSITIONS

Self-manoeuvring   Push back

③   Final A/C alignment known   3

③   unknown   3

Approximate parking area   3

MISCELLANEOUS

Obstructions { Single unlit △   Multi- unlit ⋀
                Single lit ⋏   Multi-lit ⋏ }

.   Spot Elevation

* * * * * * * * *   Lead in lights

★   Identification Beacon/Aerodrome Beacon

✿   Obstruction light on high ground

◄ ◄ ◄ ◄   Ground Marking Arrows

Wind Indicator Unlit/Lit

Landing Indicator Unlit/Lit

▷—A   Runway Visual Range Observation Site

x———x———   Perimeter Fence

— — — —   Light Aircraft Landing Area or Seaplane Alighting Area

© BRITISH AIRWAYS *AERAD*

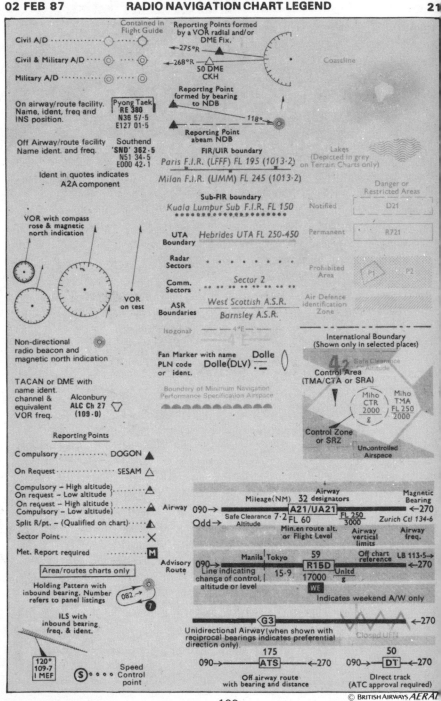